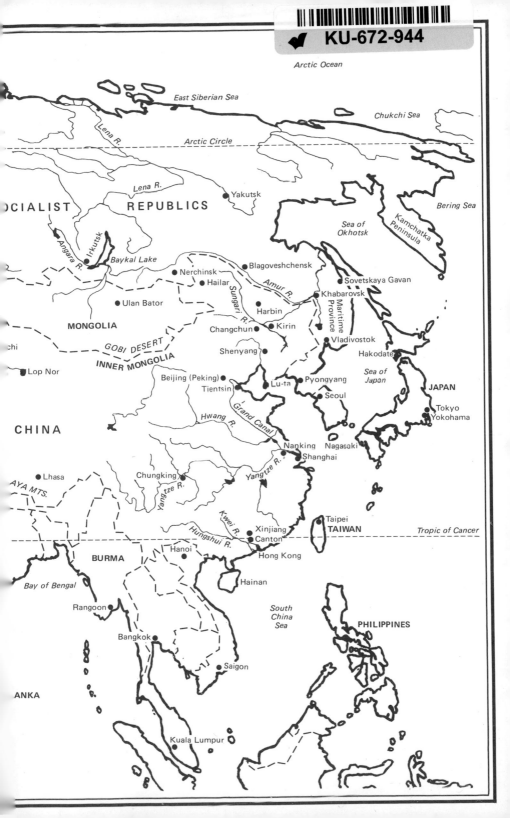

Arctic Ocean

East Siberian Sea

Chukchi Sea

Lena R.

Arctic Circle

Lena R.

Yakutsk

Bering Sea

OCIALIST   REPUBLICS

Kamchatka Peninsula

Sea of Okhotsk

Angara R.

Irkutsk

Baykal Lake

Nerchinsk

Blagoveshchensk

Amur R.

Sovetskaya Gavan

Hailar

Sungari R.

Khabarovsk

Maritime Province

Ulan Bator

Harbin

MONGOLIA

Changchun

Kirin

Vladivostok

Shenyang

Hakodate

chi

GOBI DESERT

INNER MONGOLIA

Sea of Japan

Lop Nor

Beijing (Peking)

Lu-ta

Pyongyang

JAPAN

Tientsin

Seoul

Grand Canal

Hwang R.

Tokyo
Yokohama

CHINA

Nanking

Nagasaki

Shanghai

Lhasa

Chungking

Yangtze R.

Yangtze R.

AYA MTS.

Kwei R.

Taipei
TAIWAN

Tropic of Cancer

Hungshui R.

Xinjiang

Canton

Hanoi

Hong Kong

BURMA

Hainan

Bay of Bengal

South China Sea

Rangoon

PHILIPPINES

Bangkok

Saigon

ANKA

Kuala Lumpur

SINO-RUSSIAN RELATIONS

R.K.I. QUESTED

Sino-Russian Relations

A Short History

GEORGE ALLEN & UNWIN
Sydney   London   Boston

First published in 1984 by
George Allen & Unwin Australia Pty Ltd
8 Napier Street, North Sydney NSW 2060

George Allen & Unwin (Publishers) Ltd
Park Lane, Hemel Hempstead, Herts HP2 4TE,
England

Allen & Unwin Inc.
9 Winchester Terrace, Winchester, Mass 01890, USA

National Library of Australia
Cataloguing-in-Publication entry:

Quested, R.K.I. (Rosemary K.I.).
Sino-Russian relations.

Bibliography.
Includes index.
ISBN 0 86861 247 2.
ISBN 0 86861 255 3 (pbk.).

1. China — Foreign relations — Russia
2. Russia — Foreign relations — China
I Title.

327.51047

Library of Congress Catalog Card Number: 83-72625

Typeset by Graphicraft Typesetters, Hong Kong
Printed in Singapore by
Richard Clay (S.E. Asia) Pte Ltd

Contents

Introduction

Sino-Russian relations both present and past are a most absorbing object of study for specialists and laypeople alike, for seldom in human history can two countries so different have become neighbours. Moreover, the importance of these relations today for world politics and for all our futures is so immense that everyone should be informed about them to some degree. Present events cannot be well understood without a knowledge of the background from which they sprang, yet a short introductory history of Sino-Russian relations has until now not been available. It is to meet this need that the present book has been written.

Assuming no previous knowledge of the subject in my readers, I have attempted to produce something useful for anyone with an inclination to read history who approaches the topic for the first time. By contrast to existing histories, I have cut down on details about negotiations and border regions and included more information about relevant general developments and the evolution of policies in Russia and China. Only within this setting, it seems to me, can the minutiae of the relations between the two powers appear really comprehensible. For the same reason, it seemed advisable to commence with two chapters giving outline histories of China and Russia to the date of their first contacts, which can easily be skipped by those who do not need them.

I have tried to give readers a clear summary of what seem to me the most important facts to be taken into consideration in each historical epoch of Sino-Russian relations, and to this end, and because there is so much more published on the later periods than on the early, I have gone into relatively more detail about the early. But throughout, and increasingly towards modern times, huge historical background scenarios and complicated themes often have had to be compressed into a paragraph or a sentence. The inevitable over-simplifications seem justified, since the reader can easily turn to many books on these subjects and it is the perspective which it is important to establish here.

The bibliographical guide at the end will, it is hoped, prove useful for those in search of further information, including history students and university staff unspecialized in the field or some aspect of it. This guide introduces and to some extent discusses the more important monographs and articles by many authors on which I have drawn, including my own work. It also makes some suggestions about background reading for those new to either Russian or Chinese history. Attention is directed to the more obvious lacunae in the historiography of Sino-Russian relations, and to periods for which a re-assessment is particularly needed.

This book is based upon 27 years of research and teaching, and its conclusions have been influenced also by travels in China and Russia including over a year's stay in Stalin's Russia, by eighteen years' residence amongst the Chinese in Hong Kong and Southeast Asia, and by close contacts with Russians since 1948. But I have tried not to let my personal attitudes intrude, and to allow the reader to form his or her own judgements. The fact that I am neither Russian nor Chinese should have helped me to achieve some detachment: whether it has, or not, the reader will best judge. More attention has been paid to Russia than China because the dynamic in the relations has come much more often from Russia. Essentially, however, this is the story of how two countries tried to promote their national interest and ideology as best seemed to them — a story to be seen in shades of grey, and not in black and white.

Note on transliteration

The pinyin system now official in the Chinese People's Republic has been used for Chinese names. Chinese pinyin transliterations are pronounced roughly as they appear in English spelling, with the exception of 'q' which is pronounced rather like 'ch' as in 'check', and 'x' which is pronounced something like an English 's'. In the final two chapters, Peking is referred to as Beijing in accordance with current international usage. Mongol names have regrettably been mangled as they usually are by non-Mongolists; they appear in Chinese or Russian transliteration depending on the source from which they emerge. A modified form of the Library of Congress method has been used for the transliteration of Russian names.

RKIQ Hong Kong
January, 1983

1 Two vastly different histories:

CHINA AND RUSSIA TO THE MONGOL
CONQUESTS OF THE THIRTEENTH
CENTURY

Today Russia and China confront one another across the longest
national frontiers in the world. But it has not always been so, for
the two nations did not even begin to become neighbours until
the seventeenth century—a short time in comparison with
Britain's relations with France, for instance. How did it all begin?
A brief survey of the history of the two peoples to the time of their
first major contacts will be the best start for those unfamiliar with
the general background. This survey must naturally be extremely
simplified: anyone seeking more detailed information should read
some of the many convenient short histories of the two countries
now available.

China took shape as a unique independent civilization in the
valley of the Yellow River in the third millennium BC. From
prehistoric bronze cultures, known through archaeological exca-
vations, there emerged a small civilized state called Xia, probably
around 2000 BC. The existence of the Xia state has not yet been
proved to the full satisfaction of modern scholarship, for no
indisputable remains have been unearthed, but it is well
established in Chinese historical tradition. It was coeval with the
first palaces in Crete, from which we may see that European and
Chinese civilizations have approximately the same antiquity. But
the Europeans were able to learn much technology from the
earlier civilizations of Egypt and above all Mesopotamia and the
Near East, which had started as early as the fifth millennium BC.
Some influences did reach China from Western and Central Asia,
but on the whole, Chinese civilization appears to have been much
more the product of its own indigenous efforts than was that of
Europe. It was the most isolated of the great riverine cultures of
antiquity.

Xia was succeeded in the second millennium BC by the Shang

11

dynasty, many relics of which have been discovered by archaeologists. It ruled over the present provinces of Honan, West Shantung, Southern Hopei, Central and Southern Shanxi, Eastern Shensi, and parts of Jiangsu and Anhui, and had a population of at least 4-5 million. It was already a high civilization, possessing an advanced system of writing with ideograms. All the world's first civilizations—ancient Egypt, Mesopotamia and the Indus valley in Northwest India, as well as China—developed their own ideographic systems of writing. The Shang dynasty already used more than 3000 characters, of which 1000 can now be read. (Today Chinese newspapers employ about 3000 characters, scholars may know up to 8000, and the entire body of Chinese literature ancient and modern comprises about 50 000 characters.) The advantage of an ideographic writing system is that different languages and dialect speakers can all read and use it. Without an alphabet they do not so readily produce written cultures of their own. Thus the Chinese characters have been a powerful unifying force, employed in the whole zone of diffusion of Chinese culture from Vietnam to Korea and Japan. The economic basis of the Shang was both agriculture and trade. The entire population was probably in some sense slaves of the Shang rulers, the members of their courts being ritually slaughtered when a king died.

In 1028 BC the Shang were conquered by the Zhou dynasty, under whom a feudal system arose comparable, apparently, to that later known in Europe and Japan, although slaves also continued to exist. Under the Zhou China expanded south to the Yangzi, but broke up into warring feudal states. This was an age of great philosophers, the best known being Confucius (551-479 BC) who laid down a system of ethics for the family and the state and whose influence endured until the present century, still underlying much of Chinese conduct. Uninterested in religion, even agnostic, Confucianists were also indifferent to science. Another very important philosopher of this age was Lao Zi, founder of Daoism. Daoism became a complex, original Chinese system of thought and belief, 'a unique mixture of philosophy and religion that also incorporated a primitive or proto-science', in the view of Joseph Needham. It incorporated three streams: a philosophy of the unity of all living things, rational in thought pattern but essentially religious in its mystical practices and feelings; the shamanistic nature worship of the uneducated people; and an attitude to science comparable to that of the Nature philosophers of ancient Greece. Later in Han times it became more purely a religion of salvation through physical immortality, but its philosophical, if not religious, aspects have been of no less importance than Confucianism in moulding Chinese attitudes to this day.

The Moists, Logicians and Legalists were three more schools of philosophy in the Warring States period. The first two were both interested in logic, the Moists (followers of Mozi) being more famous for a doctrine of universal love, elements of which too, in the opinion of Needham at least, were later incorporated into Confucianism, whilst the Legalists stressed increasing the power of kingship and reducing that of the upper class, to overcome the disastrous feudal wars. The range of philosophical thought of ancient China was in Needham's opinion comparable to that of ancient Greece. It gave rise to an indigenous Chinese science and mathematics, but never to a decisive breakthrough in either, though Chinese technology rose to a higher level than that of Europe before the Industrial Revolution, transmitting a large number of inventions to Europe or providing the inspiration for their development there.

Chinese civilization has in general seemed to outsiders at least to be more practical, one might almost say more sociological, in its preoccupations than that of India, Islam or Europe. If the keynote of Indian and Middle Eastern thought was religious, and that of Europe from the Renaissance onwards became distinguished by a frenetic quest for intellectually satisfying truth, then Chinese thinkers tended to be more concerned with a search for the right way of living and the maintenance of social and political harmony amongst men. Chinese science under the Han became a secret, underground activity associated with plotting against the reigning dynasty, and ultimately fell victim to the priority need to preserve the body politic intact. It is possible, though this idea has not been investigated much by scholars, that the use of characters instead of an alphabet also produced a different effect on the development of thought in China.

Fragmented Zhou China was united between 256 and 221 BC by the kings of the state of Chin, one of whom became known to history as China's first unifier, taking the title of first emperor (Shi Huang Di) in 221 BC. Under his harsh rule the written language, of which many versions existed, was made uniform, weights and measures standardised, feudalism abolished and the whole system of government centralised under the one emperor. Since that time China has been always, with relatively short interruptions, a great unified state. Although the Chin dynasty ruled over the entirety of China only for some fifteen years, it accomplished a work of everlasting importance. A high price was paid for this, however, in the destruction of all but Legalist books by order of the first emperor.

After the tyrannical Chin came the Han dynasty (200 BC–200 AD). In this period the books of the other philosophical schools were laboriously reconstructed from memory and hidden fragments, but much was lost. Confucianism became the dominant philosophy of the throne, the bureaucracy and the upper class, encouraging an attitude of virtual agnosticism similar to that of sophisticated Romans, or Europeans of the present time. Confucianism helped to cement the unity of China by promoting obedience and harmony, but it was inimical to the development of science and religion, indeed essentially uninterested in either.

Although the feudal system was partly restored and some slaves continued to exist, the social basis of the nation was now a free peasantry, either owning their land or tenants of a new gentry landowning class. This remained the basic social structure of China until the twentieth century, concomitantly with the persistence till the eighteenth century at least of some slave-owning, of outcaste groups and other feudal survivals, and with partial relapses into more typical seigneurial institutions at certain times and certain places.

In the broad Marxist definition of feudalism, the Chinese situation from the Han to the Communist period is considered feudal. In the non-Marxist use of the term, which takes the Western European and Japanese medieval feudal systems as definitive models, the Chinese situation was not true feudalism, but rather a centralised state with strongly feudal social and economic survivals.

With its gentry society, its highly sophisticated, centralised bureaucratic government, and ideographic standardised official writing system uniting all the various Chinese sub-groups and a number of neighbouring states in one great culture group, the Han empire was in some ways much more advanced than its contemporary the Roman empire. It was in Han times that the traditional Chinese view of the world order was laid down. Surrounded than only by less-developed peoples, China appeared to its inhabitants as the one and only civilization. It was not conceived in theory that any non-Chinese ruler could be the equal of the Chinese emperor, or that the rulers of other countries could have relations with him save in the capacity of his vassals. In practice however the Chinese were flexible and in case of need occasionally did treat with other rulers as if they were equal.

After the collapse of the Han dynasty in the third century AD China suffered for three centuries and more a period of disunion comparable in some ways to the Dark Ages in Western Europe after the fall of Rome. But the breakdown in China was not nearly so complete, although there was a drastic economic decline with the disappearance of gold coinage and partial reversion to a natural economy, and much of the north fell under the control of the tribal nomads who had harried it for centuries and were to turn against Europe in the fifth and sixth centuries. During this period Mahayana and Hinayana Buddhism were introduced to China from India and both forms found support. The Mahayana in particular won many adherents in the lower classes as a religion of salvation with a stronger appeal than the less organised native Daoism.

In the sixth century, China was re-unified again under the short-lived Sui dynasty (581–618 AD), remarkable amongst other things for the completion of the Grand Canal linking the Yellow River and the Yangzi. Under the ensuring Tang (618–906 AD), traditional China attained its greatest glory and came to cover most of the present territory of China except for Taiwan, Manchuria and Inner Mongolia. At this time it was the world's most brilliant civilization by far, eclipsing in culture, inventiveness and wealth the contemporary Byzantine empire in Europe, the divided states of the Indian sub-continent, and even the Islamic civilization. To mention some of the highlights, recruitment to the civil service in Tang China was by examination, woodblock printing of books became common by 770 AD, and painting, poetry and craftsmanship including porcelain attained a high level.

After the Tang, the two Sung dynasties (960–1179) which succeeded it saw the further advance of learning and culture, despite the fact that parts of North China again fell under nomad rule. The Sung dynasties witnessed a great burst of intellectual activity, although more turned inward towards old Chinese traditions, which gave rise to the so-called amalgam of Confucian and Buddhist thought known as Neo-Confucianism. In reality this was a brilliant departure from either of its progenitors and created largely by the genius of the philosopher Zhu Xi. Economic development now began to trend in the direction of capitalism and a scientific and industrial revolution. Between the tenth and fourteenth centuries China, in the words of Mark Elvin, 'approached the threshold of a systematic experimental investigation of nature, and created the world's first mechanized industry'. Early forms of capitalism appeared in the towns, and there was the start of an agricultural revolution with new methods of cultivation and new crops. There was a growth of trade and towns, and a rise in the number and importance of merchants and other middle-class groups, so that in this age, if not earlier, the outstanding business ability of the Chinese became well established. At the same time, under the Sung, there was a recrudescence of feudal-type manorial farming using unfree labour (a phenomenon similar to that seen in Russia and Eastern Europe in the seventeenth and eighteenth centuries under comparable conditions of an expanding money economy and serf-ownership). The practice of binding girls' feet also began in this period.

Yet all this did not lead to continuing radical change, but slowed up in a prolongation of the traditional Chinese state and economy. Various reasons have been advanced for this. One is that industrialisation did not take place because intensive agriculture in China could keep alive far more people than Europe's agriculture could on the eve of its Industrial Revolution. There was therefore no need in China to replace people by machines for heavy labour (Mark Elvin). Another reason suggested is the hostility of the bureaucracy to the rise of economic activities it could not control (Joseph Needham). Yet another reason may have been the secretive nature of the scientific and inventive tradition in China, which in the Sung and later dynasties, no less than in the Zhou and the Han, often considered new discoveries as family treasures to be kept hidden from rivals. Certainly a contributory cause of the abortion of the scientific and industrial revolution was the conquest of China in the thirteenth century by the Mongols. As the Mongols also conquered Russia in the same period, this will be a suitable point for us to leave China for the time being and trace the history of Russia in outline to the moment when both countries fell to the hordes of Genghiz Khan.

By contrast to China, Russia was not a unique civilization but a branch of European civilization, having like other parts of Europe its own original features and special cultural achievements yet with its roots in the common European heritage of ancient Greece and Rome and Christianity. To be more precise, the earliest Russian state well known to historians was a cultural protege of Byzantium, the eastern half of the Rome Empire which survived after the fall of Rome for another thousand years until the fifteenth century. Just as the Northern Chinese on the Yellow River gradually brought all of modern China into their civilization, so was all Europe gradually civilized from the first European cultural bases of Greece and later Rome.

In the ninth century AD the Russian tribes were united under a dynasty of Viking origin, with their capital at Kiev on the Dnieper. This state reached from the Gulf of Finland in the north to the south of Kiev, and at its widest extent from near the confluence of the Oka and Volga in the northeast to the Carpathians. There was even an outpost in the North Caucasus at one time. The earliest firm date in the Russian chronicles is 862 AD. This first Russian state showed some features in common with the earliest Chinese states of Xia and Shang nearly 3000 years before. It was a state of tribes that slowly lost their identity in a common Russian nationality. Its basis was 'burn and clear' agriculture like that of the early Chinese; slavery existed and serfdom was beginning to develop. Trade, as in Shang China, was very important, bringing a rapid accumulation of wealth. Yet it is one's impression that the Russians of that time, just like the contemporary Anglo-Saxons in England, had hardly reached a stage where by their own efforts they could have produced a civilization. The Kievan rulers were mostly warriors who spent their time in ceaseless fighting. Kiev Russia, like Anglo-Saxon England and Northern and Eastern Europe in general, achieved rapid progress by borrowing from the neighbouring civilized centres of Southern Europe, rather than having to pull itself up by its own bootstraps like Bronze Age China.

Kiev lay on the major east–west and north–south trade routes from Western and Northern Europe to Byzantium and the Middle East. It channelled Scandinavian and Central European raw materials via the Dnieper to Byzantium and via the numerous other Russian rivers and their portages to the Caspian Sea, Iran and the Islamic world, channelling back luxury products from these high-cultural zones.

Another similarity with ancient China lay in trouble with the nomads. Kiev was in the so-called Parkland Zone of European Russia, to the south of which are the vast Eurasian plains or steppes which stretch from Hungary to Mongolia, roamed over since Neolithic times by tribes of horse-riding nomads who made war on the settled agricultural peoples on whom they bordered. So Kievan Russians like the Chinese down the ages fought ceaseless wars with the neighbouring people of the steppes, who at this period were of Turkic race.

Institutionally, Kiev Russia had far more in common with other parts of Europe than with Shang China. In the Kiev state there were three centres of power, the main one being the princes of the royal family, who divided the country amongst themselves according to a complicated, semi-feudal system whereby the desirability of all parts of the country was graded, the better seats going to the elder brothers and Kiev itself to the eldest. Upon the death of the latter, all moved up one place. (Shang China also had a complicated inheritance system to the throne, through elder to younger brothers, thence to sons and nephews.) Aside from the princes, however, some power also resided in the prince's senior retainers and the rising upper class of landowners, whose opinions had to be consulted in council by the princes. Lastly, in the larger towns at least, there was an assembly of the townsmen, or heads of families, known as the *veche*.

It was genuine appreciation of higher forms of religious knowledge that perhaps prompted some early Russians to accept Christianity from Greek missionaries, but when the swashbuckling Grand Prince Vladimir was converted in 988 and made all his subjects follow him, we may suspect that the church had succeeded at least partly becuase of the lure of the higher civilization to which it gave access. Conversion, for a ruler at that time, was equivalent to gaining a membership card to the club of civilized Europe. At this period the Christian church in Europe was still officially undivided, yet already considerable differences of attitude and practice had arisen between its Roman and Byzantine halves. The acceptance of Eastern Christianity laid the still rather primitive Russians wide open to Byzantine culture. It brought them an alphabet, based on the Greek one, and all the sophisticated knowledge of the Eastern Roman empire.

Byzantine Christianity, coming to the Russians at a more impressionable stage in their development than that of the Chinese when reached by Buddhism, took a far stronger hold on them than Buddhism did in China. Gradually absorbing or driving out the old worship of nature gods, it acquired as great a grip on the Russian mind as Roman Christianity did in Western Europe. Polygamy was early abolished, as in the rest of Europe, with immeasurable benefit to women's position. The outward forms of Orthodox worship, so rich in music and dignity, and its basic central message won wide acceptance, even if the message was too hard for many to follow. Byzantine architecture and art forms were also readily adopted, but Greek thought, on the other hand, was difficult for a people only just emerging from tribalism to absorb, so that little impression was made by it.

By the eleventh century Kiev had reached its zenith as a flourishing city with a cathedral and by tradition 40 churches and eight markets. The royal family intermarried with many European royal houses, and the state was an integral part of European civilization. Like many early states, however, it did not last long. Such states are often inherently unstable because of the absence of central government institutions, difficulty of communications and the general proclivity of all the male populace to fighting. Internal strife was probably the main cause of Kiev's swift decline from the mid-eleventh century. Endless wars between the princes over succession invited endless attacks from the steppe nomads, and the people began to flee away to the west and southwest where they fell under Polish rule, or into the forests of the northeast where new Russian principalities were formed. The grand prince of Kiev lost his predominant position and by the twelfth century Russia was divided under many independent petty princes. Another reason partly causing the decline, and partly caused by it, was the fall-off in trade, for the Crusades (First Crusade 1096) opened new and quicker sea routes to the Near East from Western and Central Europe, of which the Italian states like Venice took advantage.

With the twelfth century a new phase of Russian history thus began, with the centre of population on the upper Volga far to the northeast of Kiev. It was characterised by extreme political division, reversion to a natural economy, and an isolation from

Europe which began to turn the Russians on to a different line of development from the rest of that continent. The break between the western and eastern halves of the Christian church in 1054 slowly imposed a psychological and intellectual isolation on the physical one. Mistrust grew up between the followers of the Orthodox church and the Roman Catholics, so that the Russians began to feel a cultural barrier between themselves and their nearest neighbours to the west, the Scandinavians, Poles, Czechs and Germans who had taken their Christianity from Rome. Although the Russian principalities were now safe from the steppe nomads, they continued to fight many wars against the Swedes and the German feudal knights who conquered large parts of the eastern Baltic coast. To the east and north of the Russians lay only the great forests and tundra, stretching away to the Arctic in the north, and eastwards right across the Urals and freezing Siberia to the Pacific, all empty save for a few primitive tribes. Byzantium, the acceptable source of cultural contact, was now in decline, briefly conquered by the Crusaders in 1204 and evermore harried and diminished by the conquests of the Seljuk and Ottoman Turks. So the Russians were now out on a limb at the far edge of Western civilization.

2 1200-1618:

A MEASURE OF CONVERGENCE—THE MONGOLS, MING CHINA AND MUSCOVY

We now come back to the conquest of Russia and China by the Mongols in the thirteenth century. In the latter part of the twelfth century these nomads had increased in number and acquired technical military information from Western and Central Asia and China itself. Every time the population of a steppe zone rose beyond a certain level the need to conquer fresh grazing grounds occurred, leading to migration and periodic attacks on settled lands. This cycle had been the cause of many earlier invasions of China and Europe: it now received its most terrible demonstration after the great Mongol leader Genghiz Khan came to power in 1206.

The savage, tremendously effective Mongol cavalry bore down on one unsuspecting enemy after another, moving with great speed over an enormous space. In 1210 they began to attack the nomad-ruled states in North China, switching towards 1220 to the west where they defeated a Russian army in 1223. Then they turned back to China, which they finally conquered in 1234. It was now the Russians' turn again, and their scattered principalities had mostly been devastated and all brought under Mongol suzerainty by 1240. The weakness of Russia and the general disorder in China in the thirteenth century made the Mongols' work easier for them.

A vast zone stretching from Hungary to South China was made all part of one empire, in which briefly all previous divisions and enmities were stilled. The Pax Mongolica was established, and in this great peace the Mongols brought the first historically known contacts between Russians and Chinese. There were Russian goldsmiths and warriors—probably prisoners—as well as Chinese at the court of the great khan at Karakorum (near modern Ulan Bator). Russian princes were sometimes forced to travel to

Karakorum to pay homage. The Mongol emperor of China is said to have had a detchment of Russian guards at his capital of Khan-balik (later known as Peking). The Portuguese traveller Mendez Pinto claimed to have met Russian prisoners or servants of the Mongols in Shanxi province of China. But these contacts were of no lasting historical significance.

The undesirable effects of Mongol rule on China and Russia far outweighed its benefits. Both Russia and China suffered deeply from the conquest. Both were much impoverished by Mongol exactions, and the national development of both was adversely affected.

By 1368 a general rising in China had brought the Chinese Ming dynasty to the throne, but the course of Chinese history thereafter did not fulfil the promise of Sung times. The brilliant indigenous civilization was still there, but development came most noticeably in literature, art and crafts, which made great strides through the Mongol period onwards, and in the advance of the agricultural revolution, which being unaccompanied by equivalent scientific and industrial progress led to a rising population that in turn eventually led to rural distress.

There is evidence that from the Mongol period the already low status of women worsened further, and that Ming China became more inward-looking. Han and Tang China had been hospitable to alien visitors, wide open to trade and ideas from abroad, but gradually this gave way to a more closed and suspicious nation. The early Ming emperors were more despotic than previous native ones had been, reflecting Mongol influence. Traditional Chinese attitudes toward foreign states were reinforced, relations with them being conducted by the Board of Rites Reception Department. But foreign envoys were well received in Peking provided they made submission to the emperor and conducted trade on Chinese terms under the guise of tribute paying.

Travel to and knowledge of foreign countries was largely limited to the contiguous ones of Xinjiang, Mongolia, Korea, Japan and Southeast Asia. Information about Russia available to the Mongols had apparently been lost to the Ming government. China's trade with Southeast Asia began to suffer competition from the newly arrived Portuguese and Dutch, but even before this, by 1433, the early Ming's great maritime trading and tribute-collecting expeditions, ranging to the Indian Ocean as far as the African coast, had been discontinued. Foreign trade was on the whole not a vital necessity because of the immense size and variety of China's domestic market. By the sixteenth century the dynasty was already in decline, with weak emperors in the grip of contending gentry factions.

In the late Ming there was some recrudescence of Mongol power. There were three main groups of Mongols at this time, all independent of the Ming: the Chahars of Inner Mongolia, the Khalkhas of Outer Mongolia, and the Jungars who roamed over the northeastern part of Sinkiang. Both Khalkhas and Jungars were to play an important role in Sino-Russian relations later. A fourth smaller Mongol group whom we shall have occasion to mention were the Buryats, living to the south and east of Lake Baikal, who were conquered by the Russians in the seventeenth century.

Although not under direct Mongol occupation as China was, Russia fared even worse being so much fewer in population and weaker in civilization. The 'Mongol yoke', as the Russians call it (1240–1478), completed the removal of Russia from a European to a Eurasian line of development. It was forced to pay heavy taxes, and parts of the country were many times ravaged. Mongol tyranny reinforced the autocratic political example of Byzantium, with which tenuous links were still maintained till its final overthrow by the Turks in 1453. It is thus not surprising that the new Russian state which emerged from the Mongol period was an autocratic one. Under the Mongols' overlordship, the scattered principalities were gradually all united by the princes of Moscow, an able ruling family who everywhere stamped out the *veche* with its embryonic idea of individual rights and representation. Moscow, founded sometime before 1147, became the capital of the new united Muscovite Russia, ruling all the Russians outside Poland–Lithuania by the time of the reign of the Grand Prince Ivan III (1462–1505). From the thirteenth century onwards until the twentieth century, the history of the Russian state arising out of Moscow has been one of continuous expansion.

Ivan III married the niece of the last Byzantine emperor and took the title of tsar (Caesar). With the fall of Constantinople (the Second Rome) to the Turks in 1453, the belief began to arise that Moscow was the Third Rome, with a mighty imperial and religious destiny. Ivan III began to reconquer Russian-inhabited territories from the Polish-Lithuanian state, and declared independence of the now decadent Mongols in 1478. His successor, Ivan the Terrible, a crazed tyrant in his later years, fought a long unsuccessful war for an outlet to the Baltic, and conquered the whole length of the river Volga from the Mongol remnants at its mouth and the Turkic people of its middle reaches. By the time he died in 1584 Muscovite political power extended to the White Sea and the Urals, with outposts far into Siberia, and to the northwestern shore of the Caspian, although the Black Sea was now under the dominance of the Ottoman Turks. By 1584 Muscovy was already a Eurasian power.

Socially and economically, however, the state was based under an autocratic monarchy on a Russian variant of the feudal institutions that had held sway earlier in Western Europe and still did in Eastern Europe. Slavery continued to exist on a small scale as in China. There were centralised government institutions, separate from the royal household administration, of a rather chaotic and rudimentary kind. Provincial government was administered by unsalaried governors who collected taxes and retained enough for their own needs—or more. A money economy had re-emerged, but foreign trade was still limited and cultural and political ties with Europe, restored in the sixteenth century, remained rather slight. There was now a distinctly Asian touch to Muscovite society: long robes were worn by the upper and merchant classes, except for riding, and the women of these classes were confined in special quarters. Monogamy however survived, as the Mongols had not interfered with the Christian religion. But to European visitors Muscovy seemed colourful, exotic and half-barbarous. Both Russians and foreign envoys were expected to perform a prostration (*chelobytie*) before the tsar similar to the kowtow made before the emperor of China. There had been little cultural development since the promising beginnings of Kiev times, save in architecture, ikon painting and craftsmanship. Literacy was rare. All the great economic and cultural movements of late medieval and early modern Europe, such as the rise of capitalism, independent systems of justice, representative institutions, universities, the Renaissance and the Reformation, had passed Russia by.

Yet a stirring of the submerged European element in the Russian polity was perhaps seen when an Assembly of the Land (Zemskii Sobor) began to be summoned. This was similar to the early Parliaments, Diets and Estates-Generals of Europe and consisted of representatives of different social classes who were asked to give opinions to the tsar, without any obligation on his part to follow them. Unlike their Western equivalents, however, the Russian classes had no statutory rights, nor did they seek any. In Muscovy the only persons with any rights were the tsar and to a lesser extent the high clergy. The first full Zemskii Sobor was called in 1550.

Ivan the Terrible died in 1584, leaving a country wracked and impoverished by his mad exactions, and the reigning dynasty was extinguished with the death of his childless son in 1598. There followed the so-called Time of Troubles, when pretenders and Poles contended for the throne. The state was restored by a patriotic national rallying led by a butcher, Mnin, and a nobleman, Pozharskii. In 1614 a Zemskii Sobor, including representatives of the state peasantry, elected a young nobleman, Michael Romanov, to be tsar, handing over power to him unconditionally without a hint of demand for rights of any kind for any class. So much for the latent possibility that the Zemskii Sobor would follow in the footsteps of its European counterparts. In the seventeenth century it was gradually to peter out.

Whilst the political and cultural pattern of medieval Muscovy was re-established under the Romanovs, the state continued to expand and take more interest in the world around it. Trade was conducted with England (started under Ivan the Terrible) and the neighbouring states, including Central Asia and the steppe nomads. Muscovy subscribed to the general European conception of international relations, namely that all sovereigns should treat one another on a basis of equality. The importance of trade was recognised by all classes, not least the tsar himself: a number of items of trade were royal monopolies. The growing burden of serfdom on the peasants incited bold spirits to run away to the southern steppes to join the colonies of Cossacks (free adventurers who developed a special identity and traditions of their own and were gradually brought back into state service on favourable terms as frontier guards and special troops). Others trekked into the forests of the Urals and Siberia to hunt the valuable fur-bearing beasts. It was primarily the fur trade which led the Russians to cross Siberia: Cossacks and other explorers hewed out the way, followed by representatives of the Moscow government. Both private individuals and government officials collected furs. All across Siberia a system of fortified log blockhouses (*ostrogs*) grew up at key river crossings and portages, since the main system of communication was by water. From these bases the Russians dominated the natives and obliged them to pay tribute in furs. It was Muscovite government policy not to treat the natives too harshly but the adventurers who preceded the government officials—and indeed some of the latter—were not always mindful of this. Fur played an important role in Muscovite government finances, being used in domestic and foreign trade for the profit of the court and as a medium of exchange for necessary imports and the financing of embassies abroad. New sources of revenue were needed by the new dynasty to restore its finances after the disorders of the Time of Troubles. By early in the seventeenth century Muscovite government power was firmly established in Central Siberia, based on the fortified settlements of Tomsk and Tobolsk.

When the Russians first learnt of the existence of China does not seem to have been established; perhaps the knowledge doubtless acquired by the princes in Mongol times was never really lost. Certainly by the reign of Ivan the Terrible China was a known fact, for the English merchant explorers who landed on the White Sea shores in 1553 were looking for the northeast passage to Cathay—the first Portuguese had already reached Canton via the Indian Ocean in 1514. Thereafter, the English Muscovy Company established regular business with Russia. Ivan the Terrible himself decided to send a mission to investigate the opening of a trade route to China in 1582, but did not carry it out before he died. In 1587 Lithuanian and Polish merchants were allowed free transit of goods to China. In 1608 the *voevoda* (military governor) of Tomsk dispatched a trading expedition to visit the nomadic kingdom of the Altyn Khan, ruler of the Khalkha Mongols, thence to obtain directions to China. This proved impossible however, as the Altyn Khan had been driven away by the Jungar Mongols.

Meanwhile the Muscovite government was made uneasy by requests from Mericke, the representative of the London Muscovy Company, for permission for English traders to open a China route through Russian territory via the Ob. In this we may see perhaps the earliest example of the Anglo-Russian rivalry that was later to play an important part in Russian expansion in Asia. Mericke was refused and Moscow took steps to secure this valuable route for itself.

In 1615 and 1616 Muscovite representatives were sent to the Altyn Khan and the Kalmuk nomads in Southern Siberia to gather information about China and establish relations with the Chinese emperor through the good offices of such Chinese as they might meet. Though they failed to meet any Chinese, they reached their destinations and reported back that China was a powerful wealthy land, rich in satins, velvets, silks, gold, silver and grains, and quite accessible to Cossack expeditions. Inspired by this news, Tsar Michael ordered the *voevoda* of Tobolsk, Prince S.I. Kurakin, to prepare a reconnaissance expedition to go direct to Peking. It was told to conceal the fact that it came expressly from the tsar or any official Russian source. So the stage was set for China, the great civilization with a population perhaps as high as 130 million by the mid-seventeenth century, to be sought out by Russia, the great thinly peopled state not yet a great civilization which had a population about one-fifth as large (25 million in the first census of 1725). The history of Sino-Russian relations in the seventeenth century was to be basically one of Russian demand and Chinese/Manchu reaction.

3 1618-1689:

CHINA CONTAINS THE MUSCOVITE RUSSIANS

On 1 September 1618 the first small Russian expedition of twelve men reached Peking, where it stayed just four days. The group consisted of seven government servicemen (a kind of feudal hereditary military status), four Cossacks, and Ivan Petlin, the one literate amongst them, who was a government clerk and interpreter, probably speaking some Mongol dialect as well as Russian. Literacy was rare in Muscovy and especially so in Siberia, so Petlin was by way of being an intellectual of the time. On his return to Moscow in 1619 he produced a detailed account of all he saw. The size and grandeur of the Chinese towns much impressed him, above all Peking itself, which he described as a very great city, white as snow, around which it took four days to travel.

The Russians were politely received by the Chinese, as if they were a tribute-bearing mission, but when it turned out after four days that they had brought no tribute, Petlin's request for an audience with the Ming emperor (reign title Wanli, 1573-1620) was refused and they were obliged to leave. Petlin was given a letter in Chinese for the tsar, which he took back to Moscow where it lay unread for some 56 years. (When eventually translated in 1675, it proved to be an invitation to the Russian ruler from the Chinese emperor to join the Chinese tribute system. The tsar was addressed clearly as an inferior of the emperor.)

Faced with a mysterious, unreadable letter, the Muscovite government appears to have prudently decided not to risk pursuing relations with China for the time being. In any case, by 1620 the Ming dynasty was already failing, under attack from the powerful federation of Manchurian tribes who finally took Peking in 1644 and established the Qing (Ching) or Manchu dynasty.

The turmoil in Mongolia, Central Asia and North China till the 1640s was enough to discourage Muscovy. A request from a boyar of Tomsk for permission to go to China was refused by the tsar in 1635, but in 1641-2 a Cossack from Tara got as far as Sinan and brought back yet another invitation from the Ming for the tsar to enrol as a tributary. This too remained unread until 1675.

In any case the Moscow government had trouble on its western frontiers, and plenty to do completing the conquest of Siberia, which proceeded apace. With the founding of Yeniseisk in 1619 and Krasnoiarsk in 1628, the whole basin of the Yenisei was in Russian hands. They had passed Lake Baikal in 1628, and in 1632 founded Yakutsk which became the administrative centre for Eastern Siberia. Maritime exploration accompanied that on land. In 1639 the first Russian reached the Pacific coast, the Arctic shores of Siberia were discovered, and in 1648 Semion Dezhnev sailed through the Bering Straits. All these were tremendous feats of courage and endurance in an appalling climate.

In 1643 the first Russians reached the Amur, the easternmost of the great Siberian rivers and the only one flowing not into the Arctic but to the Pacific. An expedition under the literate V.D. Poiarkov was dispatched southeastwards from Yakutsk in July 1643, seeking for fresh tribes on whom to levy tribute of furs, and also silver and other metals and grain. They found the Amur and sailed down it to the sea, wintering at the river's mouth in 1644-45, and then went up the coast of the Sea of Okhotsk to the Ulya river, thence overland back to Yakutsk. Apparently they did not learn of the tributary relations existing since 1644 between the Manchus and several tribes of south-bank Amur natives, whom they alienated by violent treatment. As a result the natives reported the Russian arrival to the Manchus.

Further exploration of the Amur was made in 1649 by Erofei Pavlovich Khabarov, a Cossack adventurer who came back with a new government-funded expedition in summer 1650. He captured the Daur tribe's village of Albazin, fortified it, and after wintering in it proceeded downstream to near the site of modern Khabarovsk, the Russian city named after him. As they went the Russians attacked the natives, trying to make them pay tribute. The hapless tribesmen again informed the Manchus, asking either for protection or to be allowed to accept Russian suzerainty in order to avoid having to pay double tribute. This determined the Manchus to rid themselves of the Russian intruders at the back door of their ancestral homeland.

And this led in spring 1652 to the first battle between Khabarov's force and a Manchu army sent on orders from Peking, at Achansk (Wuchala). It was a victory for the Russians. Following a mutiny by Khabarov's men, a Muscovite official was sent out to the Amur, arriving in summer 1653, and appointed a new head for the settlement.

Poiarkov's and Khabarov's adventures on the Amur, which so strongly recall the exploits of Spanish conquistadores and English buccaneers in the New World, had taken place at a time of stress in the European heartland of Muscovy. Trade suffered through rebellions of the townspeople in 1648–52 and epidemics of the Black Death. As a response to this, most of the privileges of foreign merchants had been revoked and European traders restricted largely to Archangelsk on the White Sea. In these circumstances the Russian government under Tsar Aleksei, who succeeded Michael in 1645, decided to make a serious effort to widen commercial ties with Asia. A trade mission was sent to India in 1651 and plans for a new mission to China were started in 1652.

Having maintained its contacts with the Khalkha Mongols, Moscow was aware that conditions in North China were now stable. The expedition, for both trading and diplomatic purposes, was organised with great care under the leadership of Fedor Isakovich Baikov, an illiterate but reputedly able man. He was entrusted with a letter for the emperor of China, proposing the establishment of diplomatic and trade relations and recounting the tsar's claimed descent from Caesar Augustus and the Grand Prince Riurik of Kiev. Baikov also had the services of a literate clerk.

The China to which the new Russian mission was sent differed decidedly from that which Petlin had reached in 1618. In place of the defensively minded, feeble, late Ming was the able, confident, new Qing dynasty of the Manchus. Its power extended significantly farther north than that of the Ming had done, encompassing not only Manchuria, the Manchu homeland, but Inner Mongolia as well. The Chahar Mongols of this region had submitted to the Qing in 1634. Moreover, the Khalkha Mongols in the eastern half of present-day Outer Mongolia were also allies of the Qing. The Qing were much more interested in foreign affairs than the Ming, unlike whom they differentiated clearly between the two crescents of foreign states surrounding China. The largely Confucian and Buddhist agricultural states stretching from Burma in the southwest up to Korea and Japan in the northeast were the concern of the Board of Rites, but the pastoral, non-Confucian areas from Tibet round to Mongolia were under the control of the newly formed Li Fan Yuan (Office for the Control of Barbarian Affairs). The Qing ruled China's millions as a tiny minority of much lower culture, so they felt obliged to adhere very closely to all Chinese traditions affecting imperial dignity and prestige, such as the kowtow and the etiquette of foreign missions. At this stage the Qing were not certain of any connection between the Russians on the Amur (whom they called Locha) and the missions arriving in Peking from Muscovy (which they called Elosi). Nor were the Amur Russians apparently aware that the Manchu forces with which they clashed were subjects of Peking, but believed them to come from a small state under a ruler called the Bogdoiskii Khan.

It was against this background that Baikov's mission took place. His instructions, in five paragraphs, ordered him to avoid all entanglements with any Chinese officials and to make no obeisance to anyone but the emperor himself, to whom he might bow and whose hand he might kiss. As well as the establishment of trade and diplomatic ties, Baikov was to furnish himself with as much information as possible about China's economic and military strength, religion and court ceremonies, and commercial conditions. Goods for trade worth 50 000 roubles were purchased by him with funds from the tsar.

Yet the whole venture was undermined from the start because Baikov sent a certain Setkul Ablin, a Bukharan merchant living at Tobolsk, ahead to Peking to announce his coming. (By this time the Bukharans were already trading between Tobolsk and as far as Soochow in China. Their identity is not certain and some so-called 'Bukharans' may have been Buryats.) Ablin was taken by the Qing court to be the Russian ambassador—or did he consciously pass himself off as such? At any rate he performed the kowtow before the emperor and was sent away with special gifts for the tsar.

When Baikov arrived in China in March 1656 after a journey of nearly two years the Chinese were not expecting him, and many problems arose over his refusal to kowtow or to drink the emperor's gift of tea boiled with butter and milk (in the Tibetan style then in vogue in China), and his insistence on presenting his gifts to the emperor personally. The Chinese tried to find out from him what connection might exist between the Russians on the Amur and Moscow, but Baikov, not expecting this, could only answer that they were free men not under Moscow's control. He left Peking on 4 September in an unfriendly atmosphere but with a great deal of information. The commercial prospects he considered unfavourable for Russia, due to higher prices in China and low demand for Russian products except for certain furs (ermine and arctic fox). It is evident that he was not a keen businessman.

Ablin meanwhile returned to Moscow ahead of Baikov by another route and the tsar, impressed by his achievement, sent him back to Peking as assistant to another envoy, Ivan Perfiliev, in February 1658. This mission, reaching Peking in June 1660, successfully delivered gifts to the value of 200 roubles (a vastly larger sum in today's terms) and a letter to the emperor, in which the tsar proposed an exchange of trade missions and free trade between the two countries. Since the letter did not use the Chinese calendar or otherwise conform to Chinese custom, and was probably incomprehensible, the emperor's advisers wanted him to dismiss the Russians forthwith, but the emperor himself issued a somewhat conciliatory edict, couched in the language normally used to tributary barbarian states:

> Although the memorial of the Chahan khan [i.e. the tsar] is boastful, proud, and impolite, nevertheless as with foreign states which turn towards our civilization, we should forgive them in order to demonstrate our principle of hospitality to strangers. Since he has sent envoys to bring a memorial this shows his sentiment of longing for justice. Let the Board of Rites treat the envoys with dinners and receive a part of their tribute. Meanwhile, we shall bestow some special gifts on the Chahan khan and his envoys, but need not send him an envoy nor return him a letter. Your office should instruct his envoys as to the reasons why we decline them an audience because his memorial is proud, boastful and disobedient.

The emperor's return gifts to the tsar included 25 pieces of damask, 3 beaver skins, 3 leopard skins, 3 pieces of velvet, 3 sealskins and 10 *puds* (1 *pud* = 16.38 kg) of tea. Ablin, in charge of the commercial side of the operations, sold some of the damask and all the tea and purchased 352 precious stones. The mission produced a final profit of nearly 100 per cent on its initial outlay.

The Perfiliev-Ablin mission showed both the Russian and Chinese rulers in conciliatory mood, looking for a way to open commercial ties without loss of face. The mission, like the Baikov one, took about four years from start to finish, for it did not get back to Moscow till 1662. Within six years the tsar dispatched Ablin again to Peking with a purely commercial caravan which reached the Chinese capital in 1669. This was an even greater financial success, resulting in 18 715 roubles profit on an outlay of 4500 roubles. Moreover, Ablin and five of his companions kowtowed and were presented to the young Kangxi (1662–1722), greatest of all the Qing emperors.

Whilst these satisfactory trading ventures were taking place, Khabarov's original Cossack bank grew to 370 under its official Russian commander, but wandered uneasily about the Amur valley looking for grain supplies for the Russian staple food of rye or wheaten bread. Unable to establish themselves, all were gradually wiped out by the Manchus in a series of counter-attacks culminating in 1660 — the year when Ablin was on his second visit to Peking with Perfiliev. Yet Russian power remained entrenched at Nerchinsk, founded in 1653, and adventurers from there began to slip back into Amuria in the early 1660s.

Not later than 1665 a Polish exile called Chernigovski, on the run in Siberia after murdering a *voevoda* in a crime of passion, led a company of 84 Cossacks to the river and built a new *ostrog* (fort) at Albazin. This famous fortress was constructed in the form of a square, each side 120 paces long, with one side facing the Amur. Tribute was collected from the natives, sometimes by raids into Manchurian territory, and 2700 acres of land were ultimately brought under cultivation. As runaways from justice, these men had an incentive to dig in; moreover Chernigovski was undoubtedly a capable leader. Their arrival on the Amur coincided with a Manchu manpower shortage draining those remaining in Manchuria away to hold down China and fight against the supporters of the Ming still resisting in the south. (Wu Sangui was not defeated until 1681; the followers of Cheng Qinggong (Koxinga) in Taiwan not until 1683.) In these circumstances the colony took root and the Muscovite government extended some control over Albazin in 1671.

But the Manchus were preparing a come-back. They had been trying to resettle the Tungus tribes of the Amur in Manchuria, to prevent them paying tribute to the Russians. Resentment at this had lead the chieftain Gantimur to seek Russian allegiance as early as 1658, and this was to prove the cause of a long-lasting dispute. Russian tribute demands were at first usually less than those of the Manchus, so that more tribes began to switch sides. Disturbed by this development, the Manchus sent spies to Nerchinsk, and the local Manchu official Sharanda invited the *voevoda* of Nerchinsk, Danilo Arshinskii, to send a representative to Peking to settle the Gantimur problem. Arshinskii accepted this offer, apparently believing that he was dealing only with the supposedly small state of the Bogdoiskii Khan. So he dispatched the illiterate Cossack Milovanov to Peking in 1670, with a letter inviting the emperor of the place to accept the tsar's suzerainty and protection!

Arshinkii's letter was no more understood in Peking than Sharanda's offer had been in Nerchinsk, and was taken to be a token of submission to the emperor of China. Milovanov was splendidly entertained and given an audience with the emperor, to whom he kowtowed. The Qing officials impressed on him their wish to start regular trade relations, on condition that the Russians withdrew from the Amur. A Manchu official escorted him back to Nerchinsk, to present gifts for the tsar to Arshinskii and transmit the request that the Russians at Albazin cease attacking the Tungus tribes of the Amur. After this, the Manchus besieged Albazin in 1671 and started military reconnaissance as far as the Amur mouth, Nerchinsk and the Lena watershed, even trying to win away the local tribes in the Nerchinsk area. But individual Russian traders managed to conduct some business with China, usually through middlemen, using a western route from Tobolsk through Jungaria.

Moscow now began to plan a really high-powered embassy to Peking. The motivation seems to have been a general wish to develop commerce with Asia rather than concern about the situation on the Amur, and was linked with ideas for a European coalition against the Turks propounded by an influential German doctor at the Muscovite court by the name of Rinhuber.

Literate men being at a premium in Muscovy, let alone those versed in foreign languages and international affairs, the tsar's choice for ambassador fell on a Rumanian of Greek descent,

Nikolai Gavrilovich Milescu (often referred to in the earlier histories by his Rumanian title of office Spatharii). Milescu was highly educated by Eastern European standards, having attended a famous Greek school in Constantinople, where he had acquired a good knowledge of Latin as well as of other European languages. After a distinguished career, mainly in Rumania but including travel and missions to various European courts, he became a political exile following an unsuccessful attempt to seize power in the Rumanian principality of Moldavia. He had then been recruited into the service of Muscovy, which as a developing country employed a number of foreign specialists in various capacities.

Milescu was appointed to the ambassadorial department of the Russian government in 1671 at a high salary. Here his wide knowledge of the world proved of great value. He was vastly better informed about China than previous Russian envoys, being aware, for instance, as nobody in Russia apparently had been before, that the Jesuits were established at the Qing court. In some ways the tsar's choice was excellent yet in others unfortunate, for Milescu was arrogant and conceited and his position as a hired foreigner perhaps reinforced his natural disinclination to diplomatic suppleness.

The tsar's overwhelming interest in establishing regular China trade was revealed in his instructions to Milescu, half of which were concerned with trade. This was to be achieved through the exchange of commercial missions in order to equalise transport costs. Formulae and methods of diplomatic contact were also to be agreed upon with the Chinese, and private Chinese merchants as well as official caravans were to be encouraged to come to Russia. There was no special mention of the Amur, except that Milescu was to arrange for the ransom of any Russian prisoners in China at not more than 30 roubles each. Finally, and not uninteresting in retrospect, Chinese experts in the building of stone bridges were to be sought to build Chinese-style bridges in Muscovy, and the letters sent to the tsar by the emperor in previous years were to be taken back to Peking for translation by the Jesuits.

Milescu's mission was quite grand. He had an escort of 6 young noblemen, 12 falconers and 40 guards, a Cossack guide and a Russian interpreter of 'Kalmuk and Tatar tongues'. This interpreter had a Russian name, but there is some indication that he might have been of Chinese descent. The mission carried 1000 roubles worth of sable pelts for trading, 800 roubles of pelts and unusual gifts for presents, 200 roubles worth for bribery and another 100 roubles worth for miscellaneous gifts and expenditure. It reached the Chinese border early in 1676.

The large embassy had been announced in Peking by Milovanov again, so Peking sent the Manchu nobleman Mala to intercept and question Milescu on the Nunjiang (Nonni) river in Manchuria. (This was the first time that a mission from Moscow had used this much shorter and better Manchurian route into China, discovered by Milovanov.) Mala, a most able man, had varied experience in high posts, and emerges from a recent study as at least a match for Milescu. For 50 days upon the Nunjiang the two officials questioned and parried each other over details of precedence and ceremonial; it was weeks before they could even agree on suitable terms on which to meet for business. In the end they had to conduct talks in a village building with doors wide enough for both to enter abreast, indicating equal status for each.

The main points at issue were Peking's demand for the return of Gantimur, the cessation of Russian raids into Manchu territory, and that Milescu conform to all rites proper to tributary envoys as China's price for agreeing to open trade relations with the Russian government. Also at stake, more precisely now than even in previous missions, were two different concepts of international relations—the European one of equality between rulers and the Chinese one of the Middle Kingdom surrounded by tributary peoples.

Mala reported to the emperor that Milescu's motives were most suspicious, since he stoutly defended the rights of the Russians to stay on the Amur and the sheltering of Gantimur. Consequently the emperor sought the opinion of his court at a meeting on 3 April 1676, which decided that the Russian should be brought to Peking for further investigation of his motives. After a journey of 29 days, full of disagreements between the two dignitaries, the Russian mission was housed in Peking under strong guard in a dilapidated compound reserved by the Board of Rites for tributary envoys. Confined most of the time in these quarters, the Russians had a dismal stay. Milescu argued strongly to be allowed to present the tsar's letter to the emperor, according to European diplomatic usage, whilst the Qing officials stuck out for the

Chinese ceremonial, according to which the letter should merely be laid on a table covered with yellow silk, representing the emperor. Faced with discontent in his own staff, Milescu finally agreed, and even at last performed the kowtow before the emperor, though he deliberately did it so fast as to make a mockery of it. Not surprisingly, Milescu failed in everything he had been sent to do, eventually being turned out of the capital on 1 September. The Qing had flatly refused to make any concessions unless Gantimur be returned and the Russians quit the Amur.

Milescu did not even make proper use of his only significant piece of good fortune. He had been introduced to the Jesuit Ferdinand Verbiest, with whom he had a number of confidential talks. Despite his religious differences with the Greek Orthodox ambassador, Verbiest treated him as a fellow European and an ally, revealing to him the Jesuits' hostility to the Manchus — they much preferred the Chinese and the Ming — and many secrets of Qing policy. He disclosed that the emperor planned to drive the Russians from the Amur by military force if they refused to return Gantimur. The Qing believed that if Gantimur returned to them, the other tribes would follow or scatter, thus depriving the Russians of fur tribute and forcing them too to go away. But this entirely reliable information was evidently not believed by Milescu, for he confidently stated in his report to the tsar on his return that Russian power could not merely be retained on the Amur, but could easily be extended into Manchuria as far as the Nunjiang!

During the mission's absence, Tsar Aleksei had died from a sudden unexpected illness at the age of 47. He was succeeded by his frail young son Fedor, under whose weak rule (1676-82) various personalities jockeyed for power and no realistic policy about China appears to have emerged. By contrast the powerful, gifted Kangxi made careful and effective plans for the reconquest of the Amur. He aimed to do this by a show of strength, avoiding bloodshed if possible, and proceeded with caution for some years because of the continuing Ming resistance in the south. Through letters sent to Nerchinsk, he again tried to persuade Muscovy to trade commercial relations against a withdrawal from the Amur; when these letters met with no response his preparations for war continued.

The Manchus had developed a new urban naval centre at

Wula on the Nunjiang from as far back as 1658. They enlisted the Tungus tribes into 'banners' or regiments under the name of New Manchus. Military farming settlements were established in Northern Manchuria, 2000 good horses from the royal stud dispatched there, and by 1686 the Qing had troops variously estimated at from 5000 to 15 000 near the Amur, to face the 1000 or so Russians east of Baikal. The emperor took a keen personal interest in all the operations.

After Tsar Fedor died in 1682, he was succeeded by the then ten-year-old Peter the Great and his half-blind and probably retarded brother Ivan, in whose names their elder sister Sophia took power as regent in March 1683, aided by her favourite Prince Vassili Golitsyn. A strong character but in a difficult position through being a woman, Sophia followed a conciliatory policy at home and in the western affairs which were always more vital than those of Eastern Siberia. Yet she planned a campaign against the Crimean Tatars. Regarding the Amur, she was probably still guided by Milescu's erroneous conclusions, though it was logistically impossible for Muscovy to bring much force to bear there. In late 1682 and the early months of Sophia's rule, attempts to reinforce Nerchinsk and Albazin achieved comparitively little. Some of the troops sent mutinied en route, and simply there were not enough Russians available. By the time the first Qing siege began in 1685 there were fewer than 1000 at Albazin, including some women and children.

Kangxi only mounted the siege as a last resort after the previous efforts to negotiate had failed. Since even the Qing themselves did not have enough Manchu men to occupy the Amur valley, they aimed to devastate the Russians' farmland and drive them away. On 23 June 1685 3000 Manchu soldiers attacked Albazin. The Russians surrendered on 5 July and were magnanimously allowed to retreat to Nerchinsk, the request for Gantimur's surrender being renewed. One group went to Peking as voluntary migrants. When Sophia and Golitsyn learnt of the surrender in November, they at once sent Cossacks to Peking to announce their willingness to negotiate with the Qing.

Meanwhile the Albazinians had returned to their old home to harvest their precious crops, so valuable in Eastern Siberia. Before winter they rebuilt the *ostrog*. The following spring the emperor sent another army against them, with orders to try to persuade them to surrender. This time there were only some 826 men in the fort, yet they refusd to submit and held out desperately until the messengers from Moscow reached Peking with the regent's offer in early November 1686. The emperor thereupon ordered the relaxation of the siege. By the time this took place in December fewer than 66 Russians remained alive in the fort. Most of these survivors fell victim to an epidemic, as did many Manchu soldiers during the period till August 1687 when the Manchu army finally withdrew.

Back in Moscow Golitsyn, his prestige shaken by a debacle in the Crimea in 1687, himself selected the personnel for the embassy to China. The chief envoy was a nobleman, F.A. Golovin, accompanied by a literate government secretary, Semen Kornitskii, and a young Pole, Andrei Belobotski, educated in Latin at the University of Cracow. It was to be his task to act as interpreter through the Jesuits, whom Moscow expected to be involved in the negotiations from the Qing side. The Qing too prepared a delegation under two important Manchu imperial clansmen, Songgutu and Tong Guogang (a Chinese related to the emperor on his mother's side). A number of other high officials and a sprinkling of Jesuits were also included in the party. Both Russian and Qing delegations were equipped with instructions specifying maximum and minimum demands, centring on the Amur and Gantimur. Golovin had a force of some 2000 or more with him by the time he reached Nerchinsk, the utmost that could be raised east of Baikal. The Manchu delegation took a guard of 1500, but had a back-up of up to 15 000 in Manchuria.

The weak Russian position was rendered worse at first by strained relations with the Khalkha Mongols, dating from the late 1670s. Relations had deteriorated as Cossacks and Khalkhas had raided one another's territory, and these Mongols virtually made common cause with the Qing. They besieged the Russian *ostrog* at Selenginsk whilst Golovin was there from January to March 1688. Then the situation was suddenly reversed and the Manchus put on the defensive when control of the Mongol tribes passed to the anti-Manchu khan of the Jungar Mongols, Galdan. The Jungars defeated the Khalkhas, many of whom fled south and accepted Qing suzerainty in late 1688. But some submitted to the Russians. This obliged the Manchu delegation to meet the Russians not at Selenginsk in 1688 as they had planned but at Nerchinsk, further from Mongol territory, in the following year, and it was here that the first Sino-Russian treaty, and the first treaty between China and any European country, was negotiated between 22 and 27 August 1689.

Three weeks of preliminaries preceded the actual talks, but there was noticeably more readiness to compromise on both sides than there had been thirteen years before. The Russian delegation at Nerchinsk went all out to impress. On 22 August they paraded their soldiers with drums, fifes and bagpipes (introduced into Muscovy by Scottish soldiers of fortune), whilst the ambassador and his staff were resplendent in cloth of gold and black sable fur. The Russian tent was decked with Persian carpets. To counter this, the Manchus stripped off their robes of state of gold and silver brocade embroidered with dragons, and went for a studied, sophisticated simplicity. No marks of dignity were shown by them except one great silk umbrella carried before each official, and their tent was plainly furnished.

All the real work of negotiation was done by the Pole Belobotski and the Jesuits Gerbillon, a Frenchman, and Pereyra, a Portuguese. These three went between the delegates smoothing out details and interpreting everything through Latin. As Golovin was suspicious of the Jesuits he tried to use his Mongol interpreter instead at one point, but the Mongol translators on both sides were so poor that this proved impossible.

Although concluded as a treaty between equals, and despite a measure of compromise in it, the Treaty of Nerchinsk was essentially a Chinese success. First and foremost the Russians were to be excluded from the entire watershed of the Amur. Albazin was to be demolished, and the frontier was to run northward up the Gorbitsa to the mountains now named Stanovoi, thence along their crests to the river Ud, which falls into the Sea of Okhotsk. The Ud was to belong to Russia, but the area between it and the mountains was to remain undelimitated. South of the Amur the frontier was to run along the Argun to its source, in Mongol territory.

Fugitives being harboured by either side—a few Russians had defected to the Manchus as well as the Tungus and Mongols who had gone over to the Russians—were to be allowed to stay, but in future all runaways, as well as individuals committing crimes on the other state's soil, were to be returned to the jurisdiction of their own country. Punishment for such crimes was to be severe. Trade was to be permitted to all subjects of both states who were provided with regular passports, but precise regulations were left to the future, the implication being that they were to be framed on Chinese terms. The very inclusion of any mention of trade in the treaty, however, was a concession won by the persistence of the Russian delegation. Nor was anything said of any Qing claim to Russian-held territory west of the Gorbitsa and Argun towards Nerchinsk.

Such was the document which governed Sino-Russian relations in peace for the next 170 or so years, a period that was to see the gradual reversal of the Chinese predominance over Russia in East Asia reflected by Nerchinsk. For the present, nevertheless, the Qing apparently believed with some justification that by dint of a blend of force with a departure from traditional methods of negotiation they had pacified the Russians and could now incorporate them into the tribute system. From the Russians' viewpoint, a remote piece of territory had been exchanged for access to the supposedly immensely lucrative China market.

4 1689–1725:

THE IMPACT OF PETER THE GREAT

On the day the Treaty of Nerchinsk was signed, 27 August 1689, seventeen-year-old Peter the Great overthrew the Regent Sophia in Moscow. During the 36 years of his reign then beginning, he wrenched Russia away from its Eurasian semi-isolation and made it once more a regular, if unusual, member of the European family of nations.

Not until 1694, however, did he take the affairs of state seriously into his own hands. Until that year old Muscovy ran on its accustomed course, with the reins of government held by Peter's mother Natalia, the patriarch and their associates. Both this group as well as the Qing emperor wished to maintain the treaty, so that Moscow refused an offer of alliance against China made by the Jungar leader Galdan in 1690. A Russian official messenger, G.I. Lonshakov, was in Peking in May–June, 1690 to assure the Qing of Moscow's adherence to the treaty. He fulfilled all requirements of tributary etiquette for his rank.

During this period the Russians plunged into China trade with vigour. A considerable amount of business was done between the delegations at Nerchinsk, and the first private Russian caravan went from that town to Peking via Manchuria in December 1689, to be followed by six more until 1697. Nerchinsk and the Manchurian route became the focus of Russian activity in the China trade from 1689 till after 1727, eclipsing the old western trade route through Jungaria. In 1692 the ruling group in Moscow decided to participate in the new market, and sent the Danish merchant Eleazar Isbrant Ides to Peking with a Russian state caravan. He was ordered to study conditions, to press for Chinese trade caravans to come to Moscow, to find out Manchu intentions regarding the river Ud, to deal with matters concerning fugitives and to ask for a Russian church to be built in

Peking for the people from Albazin. He was not told to ask for trade regulations to be made, presumably in the hope that the Russians would be left as unfettered as possible.

Ides was handsomely treated in Peking when he arrived in 1693, being given at least five audiences with the emperor, at all of which he kowtowed. The emperor was very willing to allow trade, but desirous of keeping the Russians in their place politically. None of Ides's requests was granted and Kangxi drew up strict regulations for the Russian traders. Russian caravans were not to exceed 200 men, should not come oftener than once in three years, and should not stay more than 80 days. They were to meet their own travelling and lodging expenses everywhere in China, but were to be provided with their own permanent hostel in Peking. Ides's letter and gifts to the emperor in the name of the tsar were rejected because the letter did not adhere to tributary phraseology, although Ides was given some instruction in the correct form such communications should take.

In 1695, three years after he set out, the Danish merchant was back in Moscow with a letter in Latin for the tsar. By this date Peter had assumed command, but as his overwhelming preoccupations lay in the west, his China policy throughout his reign was concentrated on the pursuit of commerce and the maintenance of peace, which coincided with the Qing's needs. There was a state of war somewhere on Russia's western or southern frontiers for all but thirteen months of the first 34 years of Peter's reign, and only the last full year, 1724, was wholly peaceful. Moreover, the vast cost of his plans for arming and modernising Russia enhanced the importance of foreign trade. During the 1690s Peter increased state control over the trade of Siberia and established state monopolies over the China trade in gold, rhubarb (imported from China as a remedy against scurvy) and tobacco (farmed out to an individual merchant), as well as fur. In 1698 he inaugurated a state monopoly over the whole China trade. This proved profitable at first, and the Chinese were more co-operative than their regulations of 1693 had suggested. The restriction of 200 men to each caravan was not enforced until 1704, whilst the Manchus accepted the cost of provisioning and transporting the caravans from the Nunjiang to Peking and provided food as well as accommodation in the capital.

In this period of goodwill after Nerchinsk the Manchu government also established various institutions for the facilitation of relations with Russia. A special hostelry was set aside for the Russian caravans, known as the Russian South Hostel. Despite the official refusal to allow a Russian government church, a church was allowed to be built for the use of the caravan men and the Russians captured on the Amur at various times, as well as the individuals and small groups which had emigrated voluntarily to China now and then during the Amur saga. These Russians were well treated in Peking, being granted pensions and permission to follow their own religion. They were organised into a special company of a Manchu regiment known as the Bordered Yellow Banner. The church and attendant buildings became known as the Russian North Hostel. Then very soon after Nerchinsk, probably in 1689, a Russian language school was founded in Peking by the Qing. Apparently it was staffed at first with some of the resident Russians. It recruited Manchu pupils only, to a maximum of 24, graduates being recruited into the bureaucracy as language experts. As the Peking Russians married Chinese or Manchu wives and forgot the Russian language in a generation or two, Russian priests and graduates of the school subsequently filled the teaching posts. The school functioned reasonably well, though never to a high level of efficiency, until later in the eighteenth century. Thus China was some one and a half centuries ahead of Russia in establishing a government institution for the teaching of the other language.

On the Russian side there was no special organisation in Petrine times for the study of Chinese matters, beyond the informal arrangements made amongst the merchants for the caravans both state and private. Yet Peter the Great ordered young men to learn Turkish, Tatar and Persian, and even established classes in Japanese under a castaway Japanese sailor. It was perhaps lack of possible teachers that deterred him from starting the teaching of Chinese, besides which his main educational preoccupation was trying to instil basic literacy in the young Russian nobility.

Throughout the whole of the Petrine period the basis of trade was Russian fur and Chinese cloth — Russian raw material and Chinese manufacture. Fur was popular in North China where few fur-bearing animals remained, whereas good Chinese cloth became fashionable with the Russian nobility and court. Cheaper Chinese cloth was in demand in Siberia, which did not produce

enough of its own. In this period, even more than before, trade
with Russia was a luxury for China, but trade with China a virtual
necessity for Russia. This was reflected in the way the China
market was over-supplied with Russian goods, causing a fall in
their prices by from 5 to 60 per cent between 1699 and 1716.
Small amounts of Western and Russian manufactures also began
to appear on the Nerchinsk market, some of which were sold in
China, and other Chinese luxury goods began to find an outlet in
Russia, notably tea, spices, gemstones, porcelain and other
manufactured items.

Nine Russian state caravans went to Peking between 1696 and
1719, with declining profitability in later years. The caravan
leaders, merchants experienced in the trade, carried diplomatic
correspondence and acted as semi-official envoys. They have
been described as the first 'Old China Hands' on the Russian side.
From the start these state caravans met with much competition
from Russian and Central Asian private traders. These latter
could go not only into Manchuria, but to Urga in Outer
Mongolia. Many also managed to penetrate even to Peking itself.

Chinese traders also went freely to Urga after the seal was set on
the Qing domination of the Khalkha Mongols in the 1690s. The
Khalkhas returned to their homeland under Qing protection and
confirmed their allegience to the Qing in 1691, thereafter
remaining vassals. It had now become a major aim of Qing policy
to conquer the Jungars. Kangxi himself at the head of an army of
80 000 men won a great victory over them and their leader
Galdan in 1696. Galdan was finally defeated and died in 1697,
but the Jungars continued to resist under other leaders. For a
brief period in the early eighteenth century they made themselves
overlords of Tibet, though this was mostly recovered by the Qing
by 1720.

The lively trade between the Jungars and the Russians was not
much interrupted even when by 1713 the former began to
endanger the Russian settlements in Southern Siberia. When the
existence of gold in Jungaria came to light, Peter sent two
expeditions into Jungar territory to search for it. The Jungars
responded by attacking and nearly destroying the second of these,
under Lt-Col. Ivan Buchholtz, in 1716. So between 1716 and
1720 Peter constructed a string of forts along the Irtysh river from
Omsk to Ust-Kamenogorsk to protect Siberia from the nomads.
This was later to be expanded into the Siberian Defensive Line,

extending back as far as the Southern Urals. Peter also put no obstacle in the way of a Manchu mission which visited the Torgut Mongols on the lower Volga in 1714 to secure their neutrality in the renewed war which Kangxi was planning against the Jungars. (The Torguts had migrated into Russian territory early in the seventeenth century, but retained ties with the Jungars.) Yet the possibility of a Russian-Jungar alliance against Qing China remained in the air. Kangxi decided to put pressure on the Russians arriving in Peking, in order to oblige the Russian government to seek negotiations at which an undertaking of neutrality could be extracted from it. The Qing were especially perturbed that the Khalkha Mongols had begun fleeing into Siberia in order to escape justice. This was the start of a problem which was to bedevil Sino-Russian relations until the end of the century, and recur in the twentieth century.

In pursuance of Qing strategy, the Chinese tried to impede the regular succession of Russian state caravans from 1717 onwards, and finally stopped them in 1719 in a letter from the Li Fan Yuan (Office of Barbarian Control) to Stepan Rakitin, *voevoda* of Irkutsk, which, however, also contained a strong hint that negotiations were desirable. On digesting the document, Peter sent Lev Vasilievich Izmailov to Peking as his personal envoy in 1719. Much more adroit than his Muscovite predecessors, Peter addressed a letter to the emperor of China in respectful tones, and omitted all his own Russian titles. He signed himself simply, 'Your Majesty's good friend, Peter', and affixed the state seal.

With the appointment of Izmailov the breath of a new age is apparent in Russia's dealings with China, not only in Peter's letter but in the envoy himself. A native Russian, Izmailov was nevertheless literate and experienced in military and diplomatic affairs, having on Peter's orders received training in the Danish officer corps (then of more warlike reputation than at the present day) and later undertaken a diplomatic mission to Denmark. Peter required him to seek removal of all restrictions on Russian trade in China, so that Russian merchants could move freely throughout the country at their own expense. The tsar also wanted a permanent Russian consul to be stationed in Peking.

Izmailov was exceptionally well treated in the Chinese capital, and was received a dozen times by Kangxi in a stay of three months from 18 November 1720 to 2 March 1721. The great emperor, always so interested in everything, seems to have displayed a curiosity about foreigners that exceeded the mere needs of diplomacy. Izmailov took great pains to avoid the kowtow, but in vain. Yet nothing much came of the negotiations, save that one more caravan was allowed to come from Russia and Lorenz Lange was allowed to stay on as consul. This was a unique concession, for not even Korea, the most loyal vassal, was allowed to have a permanent representative in Peking. But Russian requests for completely free trade were as unacceptable to the Qing as such demands were to be later, or indeed as free trade for foreigners had been in Muscovy and still was in Petrine Russia — though free *travel*, as opposed to free trade, was allowed to foreigners in Russia from the seventeenth century and a number of foreigners did obtain permission to trade and even to hold lucrative monopolies. The Manchu officials also hinted to Izmailov at the need to settle the Mongol frontier with Siberia.

Lange's position as consul was soon fouled up by Mongol problems. Even before Izmailov left, a new batch of more than 700 Mongols was reported to have fled from Qing jurisdiction into Russian. Lange was forced to reside in the rickety Russian South Hostel, now so dilapidated that one night a wind-storm blew down one of the walls of his bedchamber. He was subjected to all sorts of inconveniences and difficulties. It is conceivable that this poor treatment also had something to do with Kangxi's decline into old age, for he now had less control over the officials who were no doubt disgusted at the departure from precedent involved in Lange's presence. When the Russian caravan arrived in 1721 it also was harried, furs being deliberately released at low prices from the imperial stores in order to undercut its business. The background to all this was the setbacks the Qing were meeting in their wars with the Jungars, and Qing suspicions of the Russians, borne out by Peter the Great's offer of December 1721 to ally with the Jungars in return for free passage for Russian gold prospectors in their lands.

Finally Lange and the caravan were turned out of Peking together in 1722, although the president of the Li Fan Yuan parted cordially with him. Kangxi died on 20 December 1722, the succession passing to his fourth son, reign title Yungzheng (1722–35). This change of emperor prompted new moves on the part of both Russia and the Jungars. The latter tried for better terms from Yungzheng, and began to play off Russia and China against one another. Peter the Great decided to regulate the frontier and fugitive questions, for which purpose he appointed Lange on 29 January 1724 to be head of a new commission to deal with these matters on the border itself. A month after this information had been passed to Qing officials in Mongolia, the Peking government sent back its consent to appoint a similar commission to meet with him. Before he died on 28 January 1725 Peter had also decided to send a full-scale mission to Peking.

The reign of Peter the Great was, as we have noted, one of the great turning points in Russian history. Although Kangxi had been aware of Peter's wars in the west, it remains doubtful if either he or his successors in the eighteenth century appreciated the significance of the portentous changes made by the great tsar, the fact that behind the smoke-screen of trade, kowtowing and Jungar trouble Russia had been set firmly on the road to modernisation.

The tsar's fundamental efforts had been directed to making Russia a strong military power. He had organised the first Russian national army, and the first small Russian navy. His decisive victory over Sweden, then the great power of the Baltic, was crowned by the Treaty of Nystadt in 1721, winning Russia her 'Window on the West' in the shape of a long strip of Baltic coast and recognition by all the major European countries as the new great power in Eastern Europe. Under Peter, Russian court ceremonials were changed to conform more or less to current European usage; *chelobytie* (prostration before the tsar) was abolished; permanent diplomatic missions were established in all the important European capitals; and the European states set up their own regular embassies in St Petersburg. This city, built by Peter's express orders on marshland at the head of the Baltic, became the new capital of Russia until 1917, symbolizing the westward-turning of the country until that date.

Under Peter, shipbuilding and many other new industries were established — all without power-driven machinery. The armaments industry was strengthened, and there was a complete reorganisation of the central and local administration on Western, mainly Swedish models. This was not very successful in such a backward country, but it pointed the way for further development.

Peter made prodigious efforts to Westernise the upper classes. They were forced to shave off their long beards and adopt a German style of dress. The younger nobles were driven into school, or sent abroad to study and train like Izmailov had been. Women were made to emerge from their Muscovite seclusion and mix socially. Not only practical skills, but every kind of Western learning was admired by Peter. Newspapers were started, books printed and the alphabet reformed. Under his patronage, an Academy of Sciences was established in St Petersburg with imported German savants, and the first laboured history of Russia that was not a chronicle of medieval type was produced by Tatishchev.

By the time of Peter's death, Russia was once more in regular and respected diplomatic contact with the Western nations, and the face of the Russian upper classes had been turned lastingly towards the west. Although all of Peter's state schools collapsed after he had gone, the trend towards education for the noble young had set in decisively, and the church, that bastion of Muscovite culture, had been humiliated and placed under the supervision of a state official. But the country's basic social and economic structure remained unchanged. Agriculture was still the basis of the economy and the power of the nobility had been enhanced by their new access to education and knowledge. The merchants and peasants remained untouched by Western influence. Peter's only benefit to the lower layers of Russian society was virtually to merge the slaves with the serfs by the introduction of poll tax — yet the position of the serfs, especially domestic serfs, was so bad that they were practically indistinguishable from slaves.

In short a gulf had begun to open in Russia between the Westernising nobility and the Muscovite mass. All this pointed towards the Russian revolution of 1917, a long way off yet, but also meant that it would be only a matter of time before Russia would be as strong on her distant Asian frontiers as she already was on her western ones by 1725.

By contrast the reforms of Kangxi had been entirely conservative in nature, directed to strengthening China in her existing mould with her existing technology, and taking no account of the inevitable military weakening of China vis-à-vis the West which this portended.

5 1725-1792:

A CHILLY BALANCE OF POWER

Although the great tsar died some five months before the final appointments were made for the new Russian mission to China, the whole enterprise was imbued with the Petrine spirit. Peter's uneducated widow, who succeeded him as Catherine I, was more experienced in eating, drinking and amorous affairs than those of state, but she or her advisers made a sound choice in putting Peter's German official Andrei Ostermann in charge of foreign affairs. With resourcefulness typical of his late master, Ostermann chose as ambassador to Peking a clever, cosmopolitan Bosnian merchant-diplomat long settled in Russia, Savva Lukich Vladislavich, whom he provided with a staff of specialists in every contingent field. These Vladislavich himself vetted, replacing some whom he judged unsuitable.

The purposes of the two sides in approaching the important negotiations were, as we have seen, quite different. The Qing government wanted to establish a firm frontier cutting off the Khalkha Mongols from the Russians, and to ensure the docility of the Russians before embarking on further campaigns against the Jungars. For its part the Russian government was prepared to make substantial concessions if it could ensure the improvement of the China trade. Its maximum aim was the opening of both countries to free unlimited trade by the merchants of each, in order to escape the restrictions of the Peking caravans. As a minimum it was hoped to get the caravans re-started. A secondary goal was the opening of a consulate, the construction of a new Orthodox church in Peking under the care of a bishop with privileges equal to those of the Jesuits, and the establishment of permanent frontier commissions. As a price for as many of these desiderata as possible, Russia would agree to the delimitation of the Sino-Russian frontier between the Khalkha

Mongols (present-day Outer Mongolia) and Siberia, the inclusion of the Khalkhas into the Qing empire, and the performance by Vladislavich of all required rituals including the kowtow. It may be noted that the Russian ambassador was also entrusted with the task of observing the geographical features and Chinese military forces in the areas through which he passed, and studying the state of Qing foreign relations.

Negotiations began in Peking in October 1726 with a high-powered Manchu team including Tegute, president of the Li Fan Yuan (Office of Barbarian Control), Tulishen, vice-president of the Board of War, and Chabina, minister of the imperial household. After six months' strenuous efforts, during which the Russians were subjected to various privations to make them more amenable (such as over a month with brackish drinking water), and a kowtow by the Russian envoy, it was agreed to confirm the provisions of the Treaty of Nerchinsk regarding fugitives and the existing frontier from the Argun to the Ud, and to demarcate a further stretch of frontier between Siberia and the Khalkhas. In return for this, one Russian caravan would again be allowed into China every three years, two new trading centres — Kiakhta and Tsurukhaitu — would be opened on the new frontier, and a Russian church mission was allowed to enter Peking once in ten years under the charge of a priest below the rank of bishop and unaccompanied by any women.

On 23 April the Russian embassy left for the frontier. The lines of the new frontier between Kiakhta and the existing Sino-Russian one on the Argun in Northwest Manchuria were agreed on the spot, on the basis of information collected by the frontier commissions of the two sides, and incorporated into the Treaty of the Bura, signed between Vladislavich and Tulishen near Selinginsk on 20 August 1727. Only thus was the Qing government finally satisfied that Russia had really ceded control over the Khalkhas to China, but almost another ten months passed before Peking agreed to conclude the main treaty on the terms agreed in the capital. All that time Vladislavich dug in his heels on the frontier, holding out for the minimum concessions he had reluctantly accepted.

The Treaty of Kiakhta was finally signed on 14 June 1728. In addition to the articles on the frontier and trade, it contained stipulations concerning the conduct of diplomatic correspondence between the two governments, in an attempt to avoid the friction that had attended this so much in the past. Marriages between subjects of the two countries were forbidden. The treaty regulated Sino-Russian relations formally until the middle of the nineteenth century and like Nerchinsk represented a substantial success for China, although it was to turn out later that the Russians had gained more from it than the Qing government probably realised at the time. From the Chinese viewpoint, Russia had resubmitted itself to Peking as an outer vassal and had renounced any claim to sovereignty over the Khalkha. As a submissive vassal, it had been permitted to continue its rather superfluous occasional caravans, and had been allowed to keep a group of priests in Peking on the same footing as Mongol lamas who were tolerated there — in conditions under which they would not breed and multiply. All Russian affairs came now to be handled by the Office of Barbarian Control, the Li Fan Yuan.

Some have seen in Kiakhta the final incorporation of Russia into the Chinese system of foreign affairs, in all seriousness on China's part and with tongue in cheek on Russia's. Mancall has interpreted it as the creation of neutral institutions, lacking precise cultural content, in order to permit a smooth *modus vivendi* between two difficult partners. Finally, and perhaps with most accuracy, the American historian Eric Widmer has analysed it as a variant of the first view, namely the Mongolisation of Sino-Russian relations. In his opinion, since the Mongol problem was Peking's main concern at the time, the Qing intended Kiakhta to show to the Mongols, both Khalkha and Jungar, that Russia was submitting to Peking in the same manner as Mongols were expected to. The Russian caravans, the Russian churchmen in Peking, and the conduct of diplomatic correspondence between the states were all regulated through the same channels as Mongol affairs; needless to say, the Russians acquiesced in this for the protection of their trade and not because they in any degree equated themselves with Mongols.

For most of the eighteenth century after 1727, relations between the two countries were governed by an approximately equal balance of power on their frontiers. This much is clear, but there has been as yet no thorough modern study of the political relations in this period, so it is impossible to write with much confidence about the real reasons behind many events.

The Jungar ruler, Tsuanggrabdan, was assassinated in 1727 and succeeded by his son, Galdantseren, who abandoned the

Tibet-orientated policy of his father and determined to raise the Khalkha and Inner Mongols against the Manchus. Reacting to this situation, Yungzheng sent two armies against the Jungars in 1729. In the same year he also dispatched to Russia an embassy of 35 persons under Toxi, vice-president of the Office of Barbarian Control, ostensibly to congratulate Catherine I's successor, the boy Peter II, on his accession, but in reality to ensure the maximum Russian goodwill during his Jungar campaign and Russian recognition of Chinese right to any lands conquered from the Jungars. Reconnaissance of Siberia and Russia was no doubt another motive. Some of this embassy, under a Manchu dignitary called Mandei, were sent also to the Torguts on the Volga with the aim of securing them as allies.

By the time the Manchus reached Moscow the Empress Anna had succeeded to the throne on the death of Peter II. She received them very graciously, spending 26 677 roubles on their maintenance and entertainment. An impression of neutrality was conveyed by her bland and vague replies to their questions, and the Russian Senate undertook in writing to maintain the treaties of Nerchinsk and Kiakhta. The Manchus for their part presented suitable gifts and performed a version of the kowtow.

Although the Torgut mission was less successful, as the newly appointed Torgut chief was well under Russian influence, in the analysis of Richard Foust the interchange in Moscow in 1731 went somewhat beyond the terms of Kiakhta. Either as a token of Peking's satisfaction, or as a measure of bribery, further gifts to the value of 100 000 *taels* (about 130 000 roubles) were afterwards forwarded to St Peterburg via the Russian frontier officials. An important outcome of the mission must have been the knowledge of Russia made available to the Chinese government. Although the relevant Chinese archives are not yet available to the outside scholarly world, Tulishen's book on his mission to the Torguts in 1714 has long been known, the gist of it being that Russia was a very large, quite rich, though barbarous country.

The Russian government was the more willing to adopt a policy of neutrality in Jungaria because of the inferior calibre of monarchs occupying Peter's throne down to 1762 — 'a procession of ignorant, licentious women, half-witted German princes and children', in the colourful if hardly precise words of one historian. Moreover, and still more important, the tide of Russian interest was still flowing west, and to a lesser extent towards Northeast Siberia. From Peter's time onwards Russia took part in the alliance system of eighteenth century Europe and its wars to maintain the balance of power. Kamchatka in Northeast Siberia had been discovered in 1697 and Russian explorers had reached the Kurile Islands in 1700. In 1728 the Dane in Russian service, Vitus Bering, navigated the strait separating Siberia from Alaska which bears his name (earlier found by Dezhnev) and landed on Kayak Island, one of the Aleutians. Alaska was found by the Russians in 1732. Trade and further exploration by Cossacks followed in the wake of these great discoveries.

Nevertheless, Mongol troubles soon soured the affable Sino-Russian atmosphere of 1731. Already in that year Galdantseren defeated the northernmost of the two Manchu armies sent against him, but was himself defeated by pro-Manchu forces when he invaded Khalkha in the summer. A further Jungar invasion of Khalkha took place in 1732 without decisive results, although there was much discontent amongst the Khalkha against the Manchus and Chinese. Peace was concluded in 1735, continuing uneasily until 1745 when Galdantseren died, after which succession troubles kept the Jungars in a continual state of turmoil amongst themselves till 1755. They thus ruined their badly needed chances of successful resistance to the Manchus, for Qianlong (Chienlung) who succeeded Yungzheng to the Peking throne in 1735 was determined to follow ambitious policies.

Without any effort on their part, the Russians' influence was extended a little by these events. Jungar pressure on the three hordes (tribal groupings) of Kazakhs who roamed the area between the Russian settlements in Southern Siberia and the Mongol territories led the so-called Little Horde of Kazakhs to submit to Russia in 1735, and the Middle Horde to do so in 1740. But these submissions left the Kazakhs still virtually independent in their nomadic wanderings, and free to return to the allegiance of the Manchus later if this were to prove opportune.

Until 1755 the real friction on the borders was caused not so much by the Jungars as by the behaviour of the merchants at Kiakhta, and by the Khalkha Mongols. These both made raids over the frontier on Russian settlements, and fled into Russian territory in large bands to escape their Manchu overlords or their own Khalkha feuds. The Russian Collegium of Foreign Affairs issued careful orders that all fugitives and criminals must be returned to Chinese territory as ordered by the treaties, but so large were the numbers involved that it was beyond the power of the thin Russian frontier forces to do so. Some of the estimates were probably exaggerated, but 10 000 yurts (families with a tent) of Mongols were reported to have crossed into Siberia by the autumn of 1731, 500 in 1732, 935 with 2150 men of fighting age in 1733, and so on. The Manchus protested repeatedly at Russian failure to return the Mongols, and the Russians complained at Mongol depredations on their territory which the Manchus could not stop. In 1735 the Russians did manage to send most of the Mongols back and were rewarded with a large present of cloth and a letter of thanks from the Li Fan Yuan.

After this the problem of stolen livestock worsened, leading to a series of border conferences in 1739–43 which ended amicably but produced no new solutions or procedures to solve the trouble. From 1742 onwards quarrels centred on the punishment of offenders. In 1744 the Manchu government started the practice of closing down trade at Kiakhta in response to a particularly strong irritant from Russia, in this case delay over the trial of two drunken Russians who had killed two Chinese merchants in a scuffle over vodka. Trade was suspended for seventeen days over this, and again broken off in 1747 over a dispute about credit not repaid by Chinese merchants; again in 1751 it was stopped three times over some infringement of regulations. The Chinese were well aware that the importance of trade to the Russians provided a useful weapon with which to control them.

Following the suspension of trade in 1753 another border conference at Selenginsk patched up relations for the time being. But now the Russians began to cast eyes on the Amur again, for it provided a much quicker link by water between Nerchinsk and Kamchatka than the difficult land route, and some exploration of the Amur headwaters was made in 1752–55.

A chance to gain access to the coveted route seemed to present itself after the Manchus decisively defeated the Jungars and reconquered the Ili area from them in 1755. The whole Jungar basin now lay in Peking's hands for the first time since the beginning of the Qing dynasty, but many Jungars sought refuge in Russian territory. A Mongol chief called Amursana who had assisted the Manchus in their conquest rebelled against them in 1756, was himself defeated and fled to Siberia with 4000 yurts. He died of smallpox in 1757, but the uneasy Manchu government demanded the return of the body as proof that the Russians were not lying about his death. This the Russians refused, redoubling Manchu suspicions which deepened further when a group of Khalkha chieftains made approaches to Russian frontier officials to seek Russian backing and St Petersburg authorised the talks to proceed. But vacillation amongst the Khalkha leaders and lack of national consciousness amongst the people precluded the possibility of successful rebellion against the Manchus.

Punitive campaigns were resumed by the Manchus in 1757 in Jungaria, and in the next two years over half a million Jungars were slain by Manchu troops. Peking's domination then reached as far as the Issyk-kul (lake), nowadays well inside the Soviet frontier. In 1757 the Empress Elizabeth, who had become ruler of Russia in 1741, sent V.F. Bratishchev to the Chinese capital to negotiate for settlement of the endemic disputes over border infringements, thefts and runaways, and to obtain right of passage for Russian vessels on the Amur, in return for refraining to back the rebellious Mongols. Bratishchev was a man of much experience in Persia, where he had spent thirteen years first as a language student and later as head of the embassy. Yet he was sent to Peking with only 500 roubles worth of gifts, and the lack of preparation and modest nature of his mission indicated the low level of interest as well as the mediocre competence of Elizabeth's government. As was to be expected the mission failed, whilst at the same time it sowed more serious seeds of mistrust in the minds of Qianlong and his advisers.

In 1758 Qianlong had the Khalkha grand lama (Khutuktu) assassinated. He moved armies into the area and crushed all resistance, reducing the Khalkha practically to a state of beggary. With the Mongols out of the way there was no more third force to stand between the Chinese and Russian empires, and tension between them rose accordingly. Russia, with her forces engaged in the Seven Years War in Europe (1756–63), now felt under a threat of invasion from the Manchus. Desperate attempts were made to strengthen the East Siberia defences. Siberian officials estimated that 35 000 troops were needed to safeguard the territory east of Baikal, but in the end the frontier troops could be increased by barely 1000 Cossacks and a few thousand Tungus tribesmen (if that). The Siberian Line forts started by Peter were extended westwards.

Whether the Manchus ever contemplated an invasion of

Siberia is far from certain. The troublesomeness of the Mongols, the severity of the Siberian climate and Central Asian interests all told against it. Peking however moved to tighten regulations for Chinese traders at Kiakhta, and direct imperial representatives were also installed on the frontier for the first time. These measures were probably defensive. But relations remained bad, with angry claims and counter-claims of frontier robberies and defections of incredible dimensions passing from one side to the other. A serious point now at issue was the erection of palisades by the Russians, purportedly to contain livestock but at places intruding into territory claimed by China with the aim of annexing it, according to one early Soviet source.

Then, in 1762, another 'Palace Revolution' brought to the throne of Russia a woman of great ability, Catherine II. One of her first public acts was to dispatch a mission to Peking, word of which she ordered to be taken to the frontier by Captain I.I. Kropotov, an army officer who was also a writer and translator of some note. But the Manchus flatly rejected the idea of a Russian embassy, and soon after closed down trade at Kiakhta again. The main interests of Qianlong appeared still to lie in Central Asia. After crushing the Jungars and Khalkhas, his preparations to invade Tashkent and Samarkand were deflected only by a rising in Kashgaria, which was put down by 1765.

Whilst Kashgaria demanded Qianlong's attention, and the Seven Years War being over, Catherine II summoned a conference of her seven highest officials to discuss China. A desire for war with the Manchus had been in the air in certain Russian circles for some time, but the conference apparently served to make realism prevail. The possibility of an attack on China to regain the Amur was discussed and dismissed. All that emerged were further half-hearted attempts at border troop reinforcement and some administrative reforms, by which amongst other measures Siberia was divided into two separate governor-generalships, eastern and western. The main Russian goal in China was acknowledged to remain commerce.

Nevertheless in 1765, for obscure reasons, the Manchus broke off diplomatic relations with St Petersburg, ceasing to answer communications. This prompted Catherine to dispatch Kropotov again to the borders in 1766, with power to negotiate on all outstanding questions. From this resulted the Supplementary Treaty of Kiakhta of 16 October 1768. Under its terms, much more severe penalties for border crimes were introduced, the frontier was re-marked in places, some of the Russian palisades in Chinese territory were removed, and Russia agreed to cease collecting customs at Kiakhta. Once again, it was to a great extent a Chinese success.

This supplement marked a turning point for the better and, although the Manchus were to stop the Kiakhta trade at least three times more before the end of the century, the two countries did not come near war again for at least 90 years. Catherine II's eyes were fixed on Eastern Europe and on Turkey, and the Qing dynasty was beginning to decline.

After a slow start, by the mid-century Kiakhta had become very profitable for Russian merchants and must have been even more so for the Chinese, who were described in Russian and foreign writings as more disciplined and highly organised. The trade continued to develop after 1768. It remained essentially private on the Russian side, for a series of attempts to regiment the Russian merchants into a disciplined company, started by Peter the Great in 1711, passing through Catherine's decree of 1775 and ending in the nineteenth century, all failed due to the passive resistance of the merchants and the inadequacy of contemporary Russian official machinery.

For most of the eighteenth century the Russian government operated an often-evaded monopoly in the import of dried rhubarb from China (re-exported very profitably to Europe), and even less successfully tried to regulate the circulation of gold and silver in the China trade. Tobacco was farmed out to private merchants at times, but private commerce was hindered by these monopolies and restrictions without corresponding benefit to the state.

The Russian state caravans with increasing difficulties continued to struggle to Peking until 1754, when they were discontinued. Foust has aptly compared them to Spain's Manila galleons. Chinese official dislike of the troublesome caravans was bolstered by the general tensions in Sino-Russian relations in these years, and Chinese merchants much preferred to do business with the Russians at Kiakhta where prices were lower and variety greater. In the main however, it was their rigid, out-dated organisation, not geared to the growing economy of Siberia, which hampered the caravans — likewise the tremendous competition they faced from private Russian and Mongol traders who smuggled with the connivance of Russian border officials.

Catherine II passed a number of measures which produced a more favourable climate for the private China trade, without ending the rhubarb monopoly and even starting a new one in Chinese damask. Irkutsk, the Siberian capital of the China trade, had by the third quarter of the eighteenth century become a dignified city of solid stone dwellings, many of which grace it to this day.

In the last quarter of the century peace was not seriously disturbed, although there were various crises. Late in 1770 the Torguts of the Volga decided to escape from Russian military conscription and benefit from the destruction of the Jungars by returning to Xinjiang to occupy the vacant Jungar grazing grounds. To what extent they may have been enticed back by the Manchus is not clear. From Russian harassment *en route* and climatic hardship a large number perished in the attempt; the Torgut themselves also inflicted many casualties on Russian towns which they sacked in passage. Their survivors reached Xinjiang and were welcomed back by the Manchu authorities. But Catherine was too concerned with the wars with Turkey on which she had now embarked to make much capital out of this. Nor did the Manchus seek to take advantage when a group of Russian subjects (religious schismatic outlaws in the Altai) sought refuge in Chinese territory in 1783. They were promptly returned to the tsarist officials.

In 1778 the Chinese broke off all legal trade for two years and thirteen days over a dispute about fugitives, and an argument about the punishment to be given to Russian Buryats who had robbed a Chinese merchant caused trade to be suspended in 1785 for over six years, inflicting annual losses estimated at 600 000 roubles to the Russian state and 3 million to private traders. Finally Catherine ordered a strenuous attempt at settlement through compromise. This resulted in an edict from Qianlong in 1792 ordering the resumption of trade on the terms of seven years previously, with a new proviso that debts between merchants should be settled annually (an immemorial custom amongst the Chinese). Each side promised to keep its people in good behaviour and the Russians specifically undertook to control the Buryats. Another new proviso was that all offenders should be tried by their own laws — earlier treaties had merely stated that they should be tried by their own officials.

Perhaps the most notable aspect of the treaty now concluded was the fact that it was not drawn up as a regular agreement as earlier ones had been, but was simply 'the edict from Qianlong' signed by the border officials of both sides. For the first and only time in Russo-Chinese treaties the wording indicates that China regarded Russia as a vassal. It commences as follows: 'Inasmuch as the Great Celestial Emperor extends his mercy to all mortals, he has sent down an edict on the opening of trade at Kiakhta, in consideration of the respectful request from the Russian Senate', and continues in the same vein. It seems to mark the zenith of Chinese feelings of superiority over Russia in the pre-modern period, and presumably was let pass by Catherine the Great because of her concern over the French revolution which had broken out in 1789 and the fact that it was concluded only by local officials.

What lay behind Qianlong's exceedingly high tone? In addition to internal Chinese reasons, to be discussed in the next chapter, it must be recalled that no missions had been sent from Peking to Russia since 1731, so that the Manchu court was presumably ignorant of changes taking place there. Contact with the merchants at Kiakhta would probably have reinforced impressions of the low cultural state of the Russians, as no doubt did rumours gleaned there of the fearful barbarism of eighteenth century Siberia. Of this Trusevich, a tsarist historian, has written: 'In general, the Siberians of those days can be divided into two groups. One group thought only of saving their lives, and the other thought more about extortion, robbery and violence that saving their lives' (*Posol'skie i torgovie otnosheniia Rossii s Kitaem* Moscow, 1882, p.224).

Nor was the Russian Orthodox mission in Peking established by the Treaty of Kiakhta calculated on the whole to impress the Chinese with the high level of Russian civilization. No account of eighteenth century Sino-Russian relations can fail to take a look at this extraordinary institution. Seven missions were sent to Peking between 1716 and 1781 (the first priest pre-dated the Kiakhta treaty), the periods spent there varying from seven to sixteen years. Normally only a few members, sometimes even only one, survived the full stint. The only independent Russian historian of the mission concluded from its records that it was a mockery from the religious point of view; the unhappy clergy, wearing Chinese dress, and demoralised by their ten-year stretches without the company of Russian women or any contact with their own people, wallowed abjectly in drunkenness, mental aberration and sexual irregularities, making scarcely any converts. But Eric Widmer has recently tried to rehabilitate the eighteenth-century mission in Western eyes, justly pointing out that it laid the foundations of Russian sinology and did, in its pitiful way, try to maintain an Orthodox Christian presence in Peking.

The Kiakhta treaty allowed the Russians to set up, in addition to the mission, a school of Chinese and Manchu language for Russians, staffed by scholars from the Manchu Academy of Learning maintained in Peking to provide education for barbarians from afar. Several Russian students were sent to Peking to study with each mission, to a total of 24 by 1794. They outnumbered the clergy and were not always obliged to stay for the full ten years, but largely through heavy drinking most of them learnt nothing and many died in China. There were, however, a few glorious exceptions. The most notable were I.K. Rossokhin (in Peking 1729–50) and A. Leontiev (in Peking 1742–45), who learnt Chinese and Manchu, and in Rossokhin's case also Mongol. They produced many translations and were employed by the Russian Collegium of Foreign Affairs on their return. Leontiev served as interpreter for the Supplementary Treaty of Kiakhta, the Manchus being unable to produce anyone as competent. On the whole, however, the Russian government was too absorbed in learning things Western at this time to get Chinese studies properly organised or even properly to pay its early sinologists. Several schools of Chinese and Manchu were started in St Petersburg and all collapsed, far more attention being paid to translations of French works on China than to the promotion of Russian sinology.

Yet in the last resort the mission proved itself linguistically if not in terms of religion, and it also acted, in Widmer's keen analysis, as a kind of lifeline, a neutral low-key institution whose existence helped to preserve relations between the two countries even through the worst crises of the eighteenth century.

6   1792-1854:

THE SWING OF THE PENDULUM IN
RUSSIA'S FAVOUR

Relations between Russia and China were carried out in low key during this period. The high tone of the emperor in the 1792 agreement reflected an unreal situation, for the balance of forces between the two countries had changed and Russia was by now the stronger polity. The pendulum was to continue swinging in Russia's favour until 1860.

During Catherine the Great's reign, wars with Turkey in 1768-74 and 1787-92 and the conquest of the Crimea in 1783 had gained Russia the hugh fertile territory of New Russia to the south of historic Ukraine (this area has been considered part of Ukraine since 1917) and the northern Black Sea shores. The first partition of Poland in 1772 had brought into Russia a substantial area of Ukraine and Belorussia that had once formed part of the Kiev Russian state. The Second and Third Partitions (1793 and 1795) gave to Russia Lithuania, the rest of Belorussia and the western half of Ukraine which had been in Polish or Lithuanian hands since the fall of the Kiev state, and the southern part of Latvia.

Westernisation of the Russian upper classes had proceeded steadily in the eighteenth century, and Russia had quickly been absorbing Western knowledge. Moscow University had been founded in Elizabeth's reign (1755). By 1792 the aristocracy was largely literate, often quite well educated by European standards. This small class had enthusiastically taken up the culture of the Enlightenment in Europe, even speaking French in preference to Russian. In the course of the century the modern Russian literary language had evolved, and the golden age of Russian literature was about to begin. The number of books published multiplied: 600 in Peter's reign, about 2000 in 1725-75, and 7500 in 1775-1800. Peter's schools having failed, Catherine the Great took up the task again and laid the foundations of a state educational system. By the time of her death there were a teachers' training college and 315 city elementary schools as well as schools for young ladies in the capital. Although the foundation of the economy was still medieval-type agriculture and the bulk of the Russian people were still illiterate serfs, there had been considerable development of foreign and domestic trade and of non-mechanised industry run by serf labour. The first state banks had been established. Russian armies had fought effectively in all the major dynastic wars of the century, and were soon to take on even the armies of revolutionary France with distinction. The population was rising fast, reaching 36 million in 1796.

Meanwhile China had entered into a curious period, one of political decay and great racial expansion. Even as it reached the summit of its control over the borderlands of Xinjiang, Mongolia and Tibet, the Manchu dynasty began to pass its heyday and its institutions were in decline by 1792. From the 1770s Qianlong fell increasingly into the hands of the unscrupulous favourite Ho Shen, who cared for nothing but his private satisfactions. Corruption spread rapidly amongst the officials, and the army was allowed to become effete. Sinicised in culture and largely so in language, the Manchus were becoming less and less effective as a ruling class. Yet the Chinese people were in the midst of a great population explosion. The agricultural revolution and absence of civil wars from the mid-seventeenth to late eighteenth century enabled the population to outgrow the land resources, reaching 300 million by the close of the eighteenth century and bringing increasing poverty and fragmentation of farms. No industrial revolution occurred to save the situation, the developments in that direction (as discussed in chapter one) having petered out with the Mongol invasion and the Ming. No modernisation was taking place, and by the time Qianlong abdicated in 1795, there was rebellion in nine provinces.

China remained isolated from the rest of the world, a self-contained, traditional civilization. By comparison with Russia the military power of the Qing armies was falling rapidly behind. If the Manchus and Chinese were not aware of this—and they apparently were not—they were fully conscious of the spreading rebellions at home, and during the years 1792–1854 this induced a cautious policy towards Russia, with great stress on the maintenance of tributary etiquette on its part.

Russia was in no mood to use its growing strength against China in this period. All its westward and southward expansion and cultural change had served to make China an increasingly remote and marginal consideration by 1792. The reputedly mentally unbalanced Tsar Paul (1796-1801) is alleged in a nineteenth-century Russian source to have contemplated an expedition against China, but was murdered before the plans had got very far. Moreover, the French revolution and its legacy added a new item to the preoccupations of Russian rulers, who from 1789 until after 1848 were to be constantly in fear of revolutionary movements spreading from Western Europe to threaten their own throne. Russia took part in the first three coalitions against revolutionary France. A brief period of peace inaugurated in 1807 by the Treaty of Tilsit between Napoleon and Tsar Alexander I (1801-25) ended with Napoleon's invasion of Russia in 1812. The resounding defeat of this invasion and Russia's role in the fourth and last coalition made it, with England, one of the two greatest European powers at the general European peace conference in 1815. The Vienna Settlement of 1815 saw Russia aggrandised with the addition of Finland, the Rumanian province of Bessarabia and a large piece of Poland, including Warsaw. Much of Georgia had been incorporated in 1801. After 1815 fear of revolution spreading from Western Europe caused both Alexander I (1801-25) and his brother Nicholas I (1825-55) to maintain alliances with the conservative monarchies of Austria and Prussia, and to continue an inactive policy towards China, in which they had no great interest. The foreign minister from 1815 to 1856, Nesselrode, was so ignorant of conditions in China that until nearly the end of his tenure of office, if not longer, he believed it still to be a strong military power. Russian foreign policy interests remained concentrated on the West, with the bordering Middle Eastern states, the Kazakh steppes and the North Pacific as sidelines. The so-called Eastern Question (the rivalry of the powers over the declining Ottoman empire and the Balkan states) occupied much attention in the nineteenth century after 1815, and in connection with this a growing imperial rivalry began to develop between Russia and Britain. A short war with Persia in 1827-28 also incorporated into the tsarist empire the eastern part of Armenia and the majority of the Azerbaidjani Turks.

Russian merchants, however, were still keenly involved in the

China trade, which took on new dimensions when tea became a popular drink in Russia by about 1800. Henceforth China's tea exports to Russia multiplied steadily. Russian acquisition of settlements in Alaska in the 1780s tapped a new source of fur to replace the dwindling Siberian stocks, and the creation of the Russia-America Company in 1799 — Russia's first imperially sanctioned, joint-stock, limited liability company — opened both the possibility and the need to broaden the base of trade with China, in order to maintain the profitability of the new company and to supply the new settlements. Russian merchants also began to trade illegally with Xinjiang, mainly at Ili (then called Kuldja by the Russians, and now renamed Ining by China) and Tarbagatai (tsarist Russian name Chuguchak).

In order to promote the chances of the Russia-America Company in 1803 Alexander I sent Count Iu. A. Golovkin to Peking to negotiate the opening of the whole of the Sino-Russian frontier to free trade, the whole of China to Russian caravan trade and Canton to Russian ships, the right for at least a few Russian ships to navigate the Amur annually and for legal Russian trade at Ili and Tarbagatai. Alexander further hoped to obtain exclusive trading privileges at Nanking, diplomatic and commercial representatives at Peking and commercial ones at Canton and the Amur mouth, and the right for Russian supervisors to accompany the Kalmuk pilgrims visiting Tibet from tsarist territory. The Manchu government agreed to receive Golovkin because it hoped that the failing prestige of the dynasty would be boosted by a performance of the kowtow on the part of the envoy of a powerful supposed-vassal. However, Alexander's bold but weakly researched bid to follow the example of the British, who had sent Lord Macartney to Peking in 1797 to obtain similar ambitious trade concessions, failed no less than had Macartney's.

Alexander also dispatched two ships under the command of the German navigator A.J. von Krusenstern to circumnavigate the globe and arrive in Canton with a request to trade whilst Golovkin was in Peking. Krusenstern's ships, the *Nadezhda* and the *Neva*, did reach Canton and do some trade but were sent away again, and Golovkin quickly came to grief partly through his own incapacity and partly because the Manchu authorities thought it prudent to test him *en route* by a trial kowtow at Kalgan in Inner Mongolia, before a tablet representing the emperor. Golovkin refused to perform this ceremony and was at once obliged to return home.

This incident was symptomatic of the widening of the gulf between Chinese and Russian notions of international relations which had taken place since 1727. The treaties of Nerchinsk and Kiakhta had been concluded at a time when European, and even at the time of Nerchinsk to some extent Russian, ideas of international law were governed by the body of legal concepts and enactments called the Jus Gentium, or law of nations, originating in Roman times and elaborated in the seventeenth century by Hugh Grotius. According to this all nations, within and without Europe, were basically equal, and in accordance with this principle it had been possible for Russian and other European envoys to perform the kowtow if compelled.

During the eighteenth century, however, the belief grew up that the European community of nations possessed a law of nations of its own based on European diplomatic custom, and that this law was the only correct one to be used in dealings between European and extra-European states. The concept of the world-wide family of nations had been replaced by the arrogant one of a European family whose right and duty it was to impose its own standards on all the rest. In this light, the kowtow was no longer acceptable for a Russian envoy in 1803 because it was not an accepted European practice — Macartney had not done it, and the effect on European opinion, as on Persian, Turkish, Mongol and so on, would have to be taken into account. Since China's perceptions of its place in the world had not changed, in theory a period of maximum difficulty in dealings between the countries had now begun.

Yet despite the insults exchanged during the Golovkin affair neither government showed any serious hostility to the other. In 1810 the Russians proposed a meeting between the governor of Irkutsk, Treskin, and the two governors of Urga. This encounter took place very amicably, but China would not agree to the Russians' proposal of an exchange of missions between St Petersburg and Peking. After this Sino-Russian diplomatic relations remained for a long time virtually in a state of suspended animation, the only contact being over the replacement of the Russian church mission in Peking.

A distinct change in this institution took place from the ninth mission (1806–21) under Ia. Bichurin. This priest so misbehaved himself in Peking that the whole mission was summoned before the heads of the Li Fan Yuan for rebuke on one occasion, but he also learnt Chinese and brought home a library requiring fifteen camels to transport it across Mongolia. The Russian government itself was now taking more interest in the study of things Asian. In 1818 the Asiatic Museum was opened in St Petersburg, and in 1819 the Asiatic Department of the Ministry of Foreign Affairs was set up. Alexander I gave personal encouragement to the members of the tenth mission (1821–30), which included the student Daniil Sivilov, later holder of the first chair of Chinese founded at the University of Kazan in 1837. Articles on China began to appear in Russian journals, showing a wider interest on the part of the Russian public.

The personnel of the eleventh mission (1830–40), the most successful hitherto, included a doctor, an artist and three university professors. O.M. Kovalevskii, a noted Mongolist from Kazan University, accompanied the mission to Peking, returning the following year with a library of Chinese, Manchu and Tibetan books. The twelfth mission produced Russia's first sinologist in the modern sense, V.P. Vasiliev. Mid-way through this mission, in 1845, Nicholas I presented a library of Russian books to the Manchu Russian language school, and an agreement was concluded limiting the stay of Russian language students in Peking to five years, thus permitting double the number to have an experience of China.

By the time of the thirteenth mission (1850–60), under Archimandrite Palladii, the mission had become a useful intelligence outpost of the Russian government. Palladii was a competent sinologist; he invented the Russian transcription system for Chinese used to this day and published a lot, mainly on the history of Buddhism and Christianity in China and on the various routes across Mongolia. Above all he provided St Petersburg with a steady flow of political reports, keeping it as well (or better) informed of the general tenor of events in the Peking government as were London and Paris by the British and French agents in Shanghai and Canton. By this time the First Opium War had been fought between Britain and China in 1842, and China had been forced to sign the Treaty of Nanking with Britain. Soon after treaties with France, the United States and other Western countries had opened Shanghai and Canton to their trade. The barren island of Hong Kong with its potentially valuable port was also ceded to Britain in 1842.

During the long period of quiescence in Russo-Chinese affairs since 1810 not only had the Russian government become better informed about China and acquired a small but growing number of skilled interpreters, but Russia and Siberia had made steady economic and cultural progress to the point where the Kiakhta trade had begun to assume a new importance as an outlet for Russian textile manufactures. Machinery was being introduced into this branch of Russian industry in the second quarter of the nineteenth century. By 1847–51 almost half of Russian manufactures, mainly textiles, was being sold to China. Yet Kiakhta alone was too restricted to handle the growing needs of Russia and Siberia for an eastern trade outlet, and trade there was increasingly hampered by competition in China from British and other European goods. Sea transport to China from Europe was much cheaper and quicker than the difficult overland Siberian route, but Russia still lacked much of a navy or a merchant marine.

The population of the Russian empire reached 67 million by 1851, and reasons were multiplying why St Petersburg should embark on a more forward policy in China, whose military impotence had been exposed by the war of 1842 and whose political decline proceeded apace in comparison with the Western powers. This could be seen in the decay of the Manchu Russian language school, which even as early as the beginning of the nineteenth century had ceased to graduate any students capable of speaking and writing Russian.

Since the late seventeenth century the Manchu government had excluded Chinese settlers from the homeland of the dynasty in Manchuria, the population of which remained very small. China's defences on its border with Russia had been greatly neglected since the start of the nineteenth century, when Peking had ceased to make active attempts to win over the Kazakh nomads who continued their wanderings over an ill-defined area between the Russian settlements behind the Siberian line on the Irtysh and the Chinese-held region of Xinjiang. As early as 1816 the Kazakhs were thoroughly frightened of the Russians, who conquered a great part of Kazakhstan between 1832 and 1854. Russian trade with Xinjiang also played a part in this advance.

On the far eastern frontier with China, some exploration in the headwaters of the Amur was carried out by the Russians in the

1830s and early 1840s, and in 1840 an attempt was made to reopen the question of navigation rights through the ecclesiastical mission in Peking, but the Chinese government took the view that Nerchinsk had closed the matter. In 1846 a Russian naval expedition under Gavrilov to the Amur by sea brought back the erroneous report that the mouth was blocked by sandbars.

In the late 1840s something of a deadlock existed between Foreign Minister Nesselrode and his supporters, still fearful of Manchu strength, and a large body of opinion in Siberia and in military, industrial and commercial circles which favoured taking some action to force China to open up more to Russian trade and to yield something on the Amur. Tsar Nicholas I hesitated between the two views, but in 1847 appointed a new governor-general to Eastern Siberia, Count N.N. Muraviev. This man was to be a powerful advocate of the forward policy, and immediately began to organise reconnaissance which by 1849 had established that the Amur was fully navigable from the sea, and that the hold of China over the tribes of the area was merely nominal.

After several approaches to Peking, in 1851 the Russian government managed to secure the Treaty of Kuldja, which allowed Russian merchants to trade and Russian consuls to reside in the Xinjiang towns of Ili and Tarbagatai for eight and half months in each year. Russian trade with Xinjiang flourished thereafter; the modern capital of Kazakhstan, Alma Ata (then called Verny), an important link in the Xinjiang trade, was founded in 1854. The Kuldja treaty was doubtless facilitated by the example of the Treaty of Nanking, but remained in the old tradition of Manchu frontier control, with the Russians still operating under restrictions imposed by China. The circumstances in which it was concluded, in the last days of the Daoguang Emperor (1821–51), have not yet been fully elucidated. A report to St Petersburg by the head of the thirteenth Russian church mission, Palladii, indicates that a role may have been played by one Saishanga, a Mongol high official who advocated seeking Russian friendship. If so, this is the first instance in Chinese policy-making circles when a case was made for this line. The same line was to be put forward intermittently during the ensuing century of China's weakness.

The concessions in Xinjiang merely legalised an existing situation and did not solve the general problems of trade or the Amur. But the settlement of these was not far off. By the time the

Kuldja treaty was signed in 1851, the Manchu dynasty was faced with the beginnings of the Taiping rebellion, greatest of the series of uprisings that had shaken it since the middle of the eighteenth century. Breaking out in 1850, the Taiping was the more dangerous in that it was a rebellion of Chinese against Manchus and their gentry Chinese supporters, and inspired by a sinicised Christianity radically different from the accepted neo-Confucian ideologies of elite Chinese and Manchus, or the Daoist-Buddhist combinations of the people. It continued until 1864, hamstringing the Manchus in their confrontation with the Russians, British and French which developed in the 1850s. The Manchus were also impeded by the declining quality of their emperors: the last competent ruler, reign title Jiaqing, died in 1821. Daoguang and his successor Xienfeng (1851–61) were less effective.

7   1854-1860:

THE GREAT RUSSIAN ADVANCE IN EAST ASIA

The next hundred years of Sino-Russian relations were to witness in the tsarist period repeated Russian attempts to bite off chunks of Chinese territory, and in Soviet times a tendency towards the establishment of buffer states or zones of influence in the same. Another feature of both tsarist and Soviet policy was to be the effort, tentative at first but growing in momentum, to establish some general influence and control over the government of China itself. On the Chinese side, the century was to be one of humiliating weakness, in which relations with Russia formed a pattern of oscillations. From time to time Chinese statesmen were to turn to Russia for material aid or political support against other nations pressing on them. But these turnings to Russia were always followed by a change of mind, and Russian attempts at aggrandisement or general control were thwarted by reactions from the Chinese themselves or by the intervention of other powers. It was in the years 1854-60 that Russia achieved its most spectacular and lasting success against China, but through the annexation of lands not populated by Chinese.

Count Muraviev (governor-general in Eastern Siberia) was anxious to make use of the circumstance of the Taiping rebellion to press on with his ambition to re-acquire the Amur for Russia; he was fearful that Britain or perhaps even the United States, the most effective maritime powers, would forestall him in seizing this empty territory. In 1850 he set up two Russian military posts at the Amur mouth and a short distance upstream, and in 1853 another one 150 miles up river, together with two on the Manchurian coast opposite Sakhalin island. It was established that the Manchu forces on the Amur were small, most having been drafted south to face the Taipings, and that their arms were very primitive — mostly bows and arrows, with a few matchlocks and outdated cannon.

Despite these moves by Muraviev, Nicholas I still hesitated to give the green light to occupy the river in strength until the British and French providentially forced his hand by making it obvious before the end of 1853 that they were preparing to go to war with Russia. This is not the place to discuss the complicated reasons for the Crimean War: the culmination of years of rivalry between Britain, France and Russia for influence over the Ottoman empire, it was launched by Britain and France (Russia did not really want to fight) and was intended by Britain to crush Russian pretensions in the Near East. In these circumstances it seemed perfectly plausible to the Russian government that Britian might indeed try to seize the Amur. So early in 1854 Nicholas I permitted Muraviev to send a raft and ship expedition down the river to reinforce the Russian posts established on it.

Muraviev's large expedition of 1000 men met with only token protests from the Manchu commanders. He sent with it a note to the Li Fan Yuan in Peking, informing the Chinese that he was protecting the Amur from possible attack by the British. Another expedition followed in 1855, and a third in 1856, all without hindrance. The Peking government neither resisted nor approved the occupation of the lower reaches of the river and its north bank. Having obtained the river *de facto*, Russia was faced with the more delicate task of obtaining recognition of this *de jure* from China and the world.

Once again Britain and France came to Russia's rescue. The Crimean War ended in defeat for Russia with the Peace of Paris in February 1856. It was no catastrophic defeat, for the British and French armies had been able to capture the principal Russian fortress in the Crimea only after nearly two years fighting; they did not go further into Russia. The defeat was thus limited, and its effects were limited in time too. Russia was obliged to give up its Black Sea fleet, such as it was, and dismantle all naval installations on the Black Sea, but within fourteen years, by 1870, with a changed diplomatic situation in Europe, it was able to overthrow these prohibitions and restore the small southern fleet.

The defeat was far out-weighed for Russia by the Far Eastern territories which the British and French victory in the Crimea enabled it to obtain from China. Freed from the Crimean War, in 1856–57 the two Western allies prepared an expedition to force on China a revision of the 1842 Treaty of Nanking, for the trading system established by it had now virtually broken down. Their aim was to have their merchants do business much more extensively in China in accordance with European procedures.

This was a golden opportunity for Russia. Declining an invitation to join in the British and French demands, in 1857 St Petersburg dispatched Count E. V. Putiatin to Peking to negotiate for recognition of the Amur as Russian property, and to back independently the British demands for the establishment of diplomatic relations and freedom of Christian worship in China. Putiatin was a resourceful naval officer speaking fluent English and French. The Qing government refused him entrance at Kiakhta and again at Tientsin, which he reached by ship via the Amur. Nothing daunted, he went to Japan and triumphantly concluded Russia's first treaty with that country, allowing Russians to trade at Nagasaki and Hakodate. Thereafter like the US envoy he joined the British and French expedition at Hong Kong.

After a preliminary exchange of notes with the Peking government, the four ambassadors backed up by the British and French naval squadron started negotiations at Tientsin in April. Putiatin and Reed, the US envoy, had no naval force of their own, but it was difficult for the Chinese to believe this was the case. Putiatin kept Russia's private Amur demands on China secret from the other envoys, yet managed to hoodwink the Chinese into believing that he had the backing of the others for them. In this he was aided by the policy of Xienfeng, who ordered that China's dealings with each barbarian envoy should be kept secret from the others, in order if possible to play them off against each other. Putiatin was also aided by a diplomatic entente between France and Russia, which lasted from the Peace of Paris until 1863. France, unlike Britain, had no objection to Russia's expansion on the Amur, and so the French envoy, Baron Gros, made no effort to probe. Putiatin was also helped by the naivety and inexperience of the US ambassador Reed, whose government had no policy in the matter and was not opposed to Russian expansion. The only possible pretender to power in northeast Asia apart from Russia was Britain, already extended to the limit by the China expedition, and so the British envoy Lord Elgin too preferred to turn a blind eye and to give Putiatin the benefit of the doubt. At one point in the negotiations the Qing negotiators did ask both Reed, and Elgin's interpreter Horatio Lay, for help against Putiatin's Amur demands, but neither seemed disposed to take the request up, if indeed they fully grasped its significance.

At Hong Kong Putiatin slipped a note to the Chinese government about his Amur demands into the same envelope as a US note about the specific US claims. Later at Tientsin he played the mediator to the Chinese, but at the same time urged a tough line on Elgin. By way of persuasion he offered the Chinese rifles, cannon and military instructors in return for the cession of the Amur territory. There was considerable potential for goodwill towards Russia in the Chinese and Manchu ruling circles at this point. Indeed if Putiatin could have averted the heaviest of the allied demands and delivered the arms quickly, Peking might even have signed away the Amur voluntarily. The arms, however, were for a future date, and Putiatin's mediation was only superficial. The result of weeks of fruitless negotiations was that the British and French stormed the coastal forts at Dagu, and forced upon China the Treaty of Tientsin, a Russian version of which, signed by Putiatin on 13 June 1858, allowed the Russians like the other powers to trade at seven new treaty ports in China and referred the Amur question to the future.

Whilst at Tientsin, if not earlier, Putiatin learnt that negotiations over the Amur had been entrusted entirely to Muraviev. It appears that Putiatin defied the orders of his own government in negotiating for the Amur at all at Tientsin. On 28 May, two weeks before the Tientsin treaty, and with the help of an awe-inspiring cannonade from his gunboats, Muraviev had induced the Manchu governor of Heilungjiang (the northernmost Manchurian province) into signing the Treaty of Aigun with Russia. This recognised the north bank of the Amur as Russian and created a Russo-Chinese condominium in the territory of the present-day Soviet Maritime Province, between the Amur, Ussuri and Tiumen rivers and the sea.

Aigun has been described by the Chinese as the first of the Russo-Chinese 'unequal treaties'. Yet in another sense it was a reversal of the type of treaty exemplified by Nerchinsk and Kiakhta, for in it Russia extracted a great concession from China in return for a small one, just as Nerchinsk and Kiakhta had seen access to large territories renounced by Russia in return for concessions looked on at the time as small by China. Tientsin was a more truly unequal treaty than Aigun, for it gave nothing in return for what it took.

The treaties were signed but had still to be ratified. To obtain this, the Russian government sent Peter Perovskii to Peking as head of the church mission in 1858. A Manchu interpreter and not a diplomat of high calibre, Perovskii obtained the ratification of the Russian Tientsin treaty in April 1859. But having learnt that Muraviev was now exploring and settling the Ussuri and sending expeditions up the Sungari into the heartland of Manchuria, the Peking government decided to reject the Aigun treaty. The Chinese government's attitude hardened, and when the British and French envoys attempted to come uprivier to ratify their treaties at Tientsin in the summer of 1859, they were attacked and beaten back with serious losses.

At this point St Petersburg appointed a clever 27-year-old diplomat, Count N.P. Ignatiev, as envoy to Peking to secure ratification and encourage the Manchu emperor to accept Russia's arms offer. Should the Qing dynasty collapse at the hands of the West or the Taipings, however, he was to promote the independence of Manchuria, Mongolia and Xinjiang with a view to Russia's acquiring them as buffer states.

Ignatiev found Xienfeng and his advisers in a confident mood, when he arrived in Peking on 25 June 1859. A small clique of Manchu princes, strongly opposed to the slightest yielding to foreigners, had gained ascendancy. Belated efforts were being made to mobilise the population of the northeast for defence against the Russians, but it was too small to be effective. Peking persisted in keeping Manchuria as a preserve for the Manchus and other indigenous tribes, and the emperor turned down a number of suggestions from far-sighted officials that it should be opened up to settlement by the Chinese.

At this time the arms offer to China somehow fell into abeyance. Xienfeng had been quite enthusiastic about it, and it is not entirely clear whether the anti-foreign Manchu princes had it rejected, or whether Muraviev and Ignatiev changed their minds for fear that the weapons would be used against Russia on the Amur. Ignatiev in any case got nowhere in Peking, and in 1860 joined the British, French and American envoys at Shanghai, where the new British and French expeditionary force was preparing to avenge the defeat of the previous year. Here Ignatiev followed Putiatin's example with redoubled vigour, urging Elgin and Gros to maximum military effort, advice which they willingly followed. The capture of Tientsin by the allies was followed by the capture of Peking itself, and the sack of the Summer Palace. When the allied forces were at the walls of Peking, Ignatiev entered the city and took up residence at the Russian church mission. Now like Putiatin he acted as mediator, yet kept the Chinese government in the belief that the allied forces were backing his own Amur demands, of which the allied envoys remained in ignorance.

The result was the Sino-Russian Treaty of Peking of 14 November 1860, which gave Russia unconditionally the whole region from the Stanovoi range to the Amur, and the Maritime Province. A considerable amount of territory on the Xinjiang frontier also passed to Russia, as it was stipulated that the border should now be drawn along the Chinese picket lines, thus giving Russia the whole of the former neutral zone between these and the Russian forward military posts. In addition, the trading, consular and diplomatic provisions of the Treaty of Tientsin were confirmed, and Russian consulates could also be opened in Urga and in Kashgar in Xinjiang. Unrestricted duty-free barter trade was permitted along the whole Manchurian section of the frontier. Frontier authorities of each side were decreed to be at liberty to conduct correspondence with each other, and the governor of Eastern Siberia could communicate directly with the Li Fan Yuan. Most-favoured-nation rights were extended to Russia in China (i.e. if any further concessions were granted to a foreign power by China, Russia was entitled to receive the same), but the most-favoured-nation principle was deemed not to apply to the dispositions regarding the Sino-Russian land frontier (i.e. other powers could not extend their influence there).

After the treaty was signed, Ignatiev renewed the arms offer with a view to consolidating Russian influence in Peking by helping China suppress the Taiping rebellion. The role of major foreign influence over the Peking government had, however, fallen to the British, who now found their anti-Russian sentiments met with a ready reception in Peking. When the Russian arms were finally accepted in 1862, after many Chinese hesitations, the British ambassador was able to persuade the Qing government to return part of them, the remainder being used by the British-trained Peking Field Force to suppress banditry in Manchuria in 1865.

In a series of frontier agreements starting in June 1861 and continuing to 1884, the new boundaries between China and

Russia in Manchuria and Xinjiang were roughly laid down. Owing to the wild, uninhabited nature of most of the terrain the marking was inadequate by any modern standard, most of the frontier posts being an average of 40 kilometres apart (on a very general estimate). This pioneer delimitation proved adequate for the needs of the time, but stored up trouble for the future.

8   1860-1917:

TSARIST RUSSIAN PREPONDERANCE
AND DECLINE

With the exception of frontier incidents, and the Ili affair discussed a few paragraphs below, Sino-Russian relations remained fairly quiet between 1860 and 1895. All the major powers including Russia established legations in Peking, and the Chinese eventually appointed a minister jointly to Russia, Germany and Austro-Hungary in 1874. But the part played by the Russian minister in Peking was less than that of his British counterpart for the first 35 years. The Russian legation assumed the political, and later the linguistic training, responsibilities of the eccelesiastical mission, which now tried on a much smaller scale to emulate the missionary activities of the Roman Catholics and Protestants in China.

Russia found it had swallowed a decidedly indigestible mouthful in the new Far Eastern territories, which proved a drain on the exchequer for many years, agriculturally disappointing and too hard of access to colonise easily. In any case, the Russian government turned its attention away from East Asia again, for the Crimean War had revealed the need for great changes at home. The lack of mechanised heavy industry and railways and the discontent of the serf conscripts had been major causes of the defeat. Alexander II (1855–81) consequently carried through the emancipation of the serfs in 1861, established Russia's first local government system based on elected representatives with a limited amount of independence from the bureaucracy, reformed the judicial and conscription systems, and launched a massive programme of industrialization and railway-building through the medium of foreign banks and privileges to foreign capitalists. The effect of this was to push Russia headlong on the path of industrialization, making her the world's fourth-largest heavy industrial power by 1914. It also introduced a growing element of disequilibrium into the Russian state, creating a modernising, liberal, capitalist wedge in tne old autocratic, bureaucratic structure of the empire. Since Alexander and his son, Alexander III (1881-94), had no intention of giving up their autocratic powers, a revolutionary movement came into being that was increasingly influenced by Western socialist ideas and determined to bring about political freedom by violent change. The end of the chapter that began after the Crimean War was the 1905 Russian revolution and its sequel in 1917.

In foreign policy Russia leant on allies in this period of weakened prestige after the Crimean defeat. Falling out with France over the Polish revolt of 1863, it returned to friendship with Prussia and after 1871 with the united Germany. In its strategy of industrialization Russia relied increasingly on foreign loans, financed chiefly by large grain exports produced by heavy taxation of the now officially liberated serfs, who were thus forced to sell nearly all they grew. Foreign money poured in, chiefly from Germany in the period 1863-87. But the alliance with Germany, so strategically and politically sensible for tsarist Russia, foundered between 1887 and 1890, partly through the opposed interests of Prussian grain growers and Russian grain exporters, partly from the foolishness of the young German emperor, Wilhelm II, and partly through the emerging rivalry in the Balkans between Russia and Germany's ally, Austro-Hungary. In 1893-94 a close alliance was concluded between France and Russia, which bolstered the tsarist regime financially and offered France vast reserves of Russian military manpower to help it face the growing might and numbers of the Germans.

Although absorbed at home, checked in the Balkans, and temprarily sated in the Far East, Russia found a new and easy field of expansion in the nomads and antiquated oasis states of Central Asia. Between 1860 and 1884 it conquered the whole of the present five Central Asian republics of the Soviet Union. The strategic and economic importance of this was considerable, making Russia quickly into a great colonial power, reversing the situation of mid-eighteenth century when China had been the dominant force in the area, and bringing a source of tropical products, including cotton and valuable minerals, into the Russian market. Tension with Britain was much fomented as Russian troops drew right up to the borders of Afghanistan, the buffer state of British India, and the two empires, British and Russian, became rivals for influence there and in Persia, and soon in Chinese Central Asia as well.

In China, the defeat of 1860 marked in some ways the lowest ebb of the traditional Chinese state — and the turn of the tide, for thereafter China began the endeavours to restore its strength and prestige which still continue today. By tacit consent of the powers, the Qing dynasty was left on the throne. The period from 1860 to the First World War saw China a field of great-power rivalry for railway, mining and loan concessions, but some benefit did accrue to it from this, despite much humiliation. By 1864 the Taipings were suppressed with Western aid, and efforts to adopt Western armaments, railways and industries began. At first there was a continuing rejection of Western ideas, but these soon commenced to seep in when the practice of sending Chinese students to study abroad started in the 1870s. In 1861 the first proper office for the conduct of foreign affairs was set up, and began to develop a considerable expertise in handling Russia and other foreign powers. A new language school, the Tong Wen Guan, was established in Peking, with branches elsewhere, providing competent interpreters in Russian and other foreign tongues. By 1895, when the next serious phase of Sino-Russian relations began, China's leading intelligentsia had become aware of the past history and present situation of Russia. Another wise and significant step taken in this period was the gradual opening of Manchuria to Chinese settlement, so that by 1895 the population of Manchuria had reached 5.7 million.

Though the Chinese demographic hold on Manchuria came to be assured between 1860 and 1895, the Russians steadily increased their influence amongst the Mongols in this period and many frontier incidents arose which were partly at least connected with the Russian advance in Central Asia. In most cases Peking took a conciliatory line in these incidents, being only too aware of its own weakness. There was one occasion, however, when China stood up to Russia and achieved some success. In 1862 rebellion broke out amongst the Muslim inhabitants of Xinjiang (at this time they far outnumbered the Chinese and Manchus there) and by 1866 Peking had lost all control over the province. From various contending leaders Yakub Beg emerged as ruler with British approval, in 1870. The latter fact was alarming to St Petersburg, which was suffering other vexations from an influx of Xinjiang refugees, who engaged in stealing livestock. Russia at that time, it must not be forgotten, was herself busy making a piecemeal conquest of Central Asia to the west of Xinjiang. In these circumstances it was fairly easy for the governor-general of Russian Turkestan to send an army into the Ili area and occupy 1224 square miles of territory between the Muzart and the Talki passes and the headwaters of the Tekesh and Ili rivers, both of which drained out of Xinjiang into lands already held by the Russians. St Petersburg declared it would return the area to China when law and order had been restored.

To the surprise of the outside world, Chinese generals rapidly reconquered Xinjiang in 1877, and Peking appointed an ambassador to St Petersburg to negotiate the return of the region occupied by Russia. Ill-prepared and inept, this Manchu ambassador, Chong-hou, was forced to sign the Treaty of Livadia in 1879, by which Russia only consented to return the Ili valley, against compensation with the valley of the Tekesh and the passes in the Tienshan mountains leading to Kashgar and Khokand. The treaty also provided for payment of 5 million roubles by China, seven Russian consulates in Xinjiang, duty-free trade in Mongolia, passage across Northern China for Russian merchants, and the right to navigate the Sungari right up to Boduna in the far interior of Manchuria. An indignant reaction followed in China and the Western capitals. In 1881 another Chinese ambassador, the able Zeng Jizi, was able to extract a partial reversal by the Treaty of St Petersburg. China had to pay 9 million roubles and cede a piece of territory on the outer edge of the occupied region, but the rest was returned to her, including the Tekesh valley, and the number of new Russian consulates was reduced to two. The Sungari demand was dropped. China had been aided by a financial crisis in Russia and indecision in the Russian government.

An equally partial success was to await the next Russian attempt at encroachment on Chinese territory. By 1894 the Russians had started the construction of the Trans-Siberian railway and were beginning to think that a short cut across Northern Manchuria direct to Vladivostok would be preferable to taking the line all the way along the Amur and down through the Maritime from the north. Soon an opportunity to get the Manchurian route presented itself, for in 1894 war broke out between China and Japan over Korea, in which China was quickly beaten. The Japanese, a tightly knit island people who had borrowed much of their culture from China in the first millennium AD, had felt able to borrow wholesale from the West too, and had modernized their institutions and armaments with amazing speed so that now they were able to defeat the much more numerous Chinese.

By the 1895 Treaty of Shimonoseki China had to renounce its claim to be overlord of Korea and cede to Japan Taiwan, the Pescadore Islands and the Liaodong peninsula in Southern Manchuria, containing the major Chinese naval base at Lüshun (Port Arthur). Important trade concessions were also made to Japan by a supplementary treaty. At this point Russia stepped in with the diplomatic backing of its ally France, and of Germany, which was glad to divert tsarist attention to the Far East. This so-called Triple Intervention forced Japan to renounce its Manchurian conquest.

China now felt in danger of dismemberment by the powers, and the senior Chinese official Li Hongzhang favoured seeking Russian help to control the rest. Inviting Li to St Petersburg in 1896, the Russians persuaded him (allegedly by bribery, but it has not been conclusively proved) to sign a treaty of alliance by which Russia undertook to help defend China against attack by Japan. Li undertook in return to allow Russia to construct a railway across Northern Manchuria to link Vladivostok with the Trans-Siberian. The president was to be Chinese and the line could be purchased by China in 36 years. It was to be built with funds supplied by a newly established 'Russo-Chinese' Bank, in which China invested 5 million *taels*, but in reality the bank was a Franco-Russian one, operating mainly with French money under Russian political control.

Between 1897 and 1903 the Russians built the famous Chinese Eastern Railway (CER), a remarkable achievement carried out in wild country with a harsh climate. A string of Russian settlements grew up along the railway and one new Russian town, Harbin, which by 1903 had some 60 000 people, perhaps half or two-thirds of whom were Russian.

In the first year of the railway construction the facade of a joint Sino-Russian enterprise was maintained, but in 1898 Russia joined in the rush of the European powers to acquire bases and concessions in China. Germany obtained Jiaozhou, Britain Weihaiwei and Russia the southern tip of the Liaodong peninsula with the ice-free port of Lushun—the so-called leased territory. At once the hollowness of the fictitious Russo-Chinese alliance was exposed and Li Hongzhang fell from power. Russia now obliged China to allow it to build a further railway, the South Manchurian line (SMR). From this point on the Peking government ceased to rely on Russia.

China was virtually divided into spheres of influence by the powers: France in the south, Britain in the Yangzi valley and Shanxi, Germany in Shandong and the Yellow River valley, whilst Russia at first wanted to claim all Manchuria, Jili province and Xinjiang. Opposition from Britain obliged Russia to sign an agreement with London limiting it to the lands north of the Great Wall in April 1899. Meanwhile, the extreme expansionists in the Russian government wanted to extend their country's influence over Korea, thus courting the hostility of Japan. An agreement with Japan in April 1898 provided the basis for a settlement of this issue by stipulating that neither country should assume political control there, leaving Japan free to develop its growing commercial and industrial interests in Korea.

Even whilst the powers were haggling over China, great stirrings were taking place there. In 1898 for a brief period two enlightened intellectual officials, Kang Yuwei and Liang Qiqiao, gained the support of the emperor and tried to carry out sweeping reforms. They were soon thwarted by the emperor's mother, the crafty empress dowager, who had her unfortunate son kept a virtual prisoner thereafter, but a decisive impetus to the movement for change had been given. At the same time the common people of China had begun an anti-foreign rising of their own, the 'Boxer rebellion'. Starting in Shandong, where the Germans infuriated people by their high-handed policies, the ferocious Boxer movement soon had all North China aflame and threatened even the foreign embassies in Peking, being rather hesitantly backed by the Chinese court. It swept into Manchuria and won support from officials in the southernmost province of Fengtien. The Russian railway builders and guards there were forced to withdraw to the leased territory with casualties. The SMR was destroyed in a number of places, and the Russians on the CER also felt seriously threatened. In July fighting broke out at one place on the Amur when the Chinese fired on Russian troopships, and Harbin was rather loosely besieged. Russia sent troops to participate in the international force, which in August 1900 lifted the siege of the embassies in Peking. Despite the desperate efforts of Li Hongzhang (brought back to deal with the situation) and the Chinese minister in St Petersburg, Yang Ru, to persuade the Russians to evacuate Manchuria altogether and hand over the CER to temporary safekeeping by China, a large Russian expeditionary force of about 100 000 men invaded Manchuria from six directions in the third week of July. By November the region was more or less under Russian military control.

But the Russian military occupation proved to be largely a fiasco. Already the railways and the ports had cost vast sums, far in excess of estimates, and to this was now added the expense of combating guerilla forces and the bandits endemic in the area. Neither the Russian economy nor its population was adequate to absorb this enormous territory. Chinese peasant colonists poured in by the new railways, whilst only a few Russian peasants could be attracted. The vast mineral resources of Manchuria were scarcely touched by the Russians, and China and other countries benefited more from the trading opportunities than did Russian businessmen.

Even the Russian higher educational system proved unable to provide the large numbers of interpreters needed. By contrast China had now begun to produce about as many interpreters as the Russians, and in addition a large class of uneducated Chinese interpreters sprang into being, mostly former servants in the Russian Far Eastern provinces which now had a substantial Chinese population. Great harm was done to Russian officialdom and the Chinese of Manchuria by these men through their dishonesty and criminal activities.

Lacking the ability to administer the country, the Russian army merely exercised some general supervision over appointment of the Manchu generals and officials in command of the three Manchurian provinces, restricting the numbers of their troops and extorting mining rights of which not much use was made. The Peking government stubbornly refused to recognise many of the concessions obtained by the Russians. The Russian railways however opened up the country to extensive Chinese colonisation and Manchuria became very prosperous.

The British, whose embroilment in the Boer War had exposed the over-extension of their power in China, concluded an alliance with Japan in 1902 aimed at checking the Russian advance. Faced with the hostility of China and the powers, Russia grudgingly concluded an agreement with Peking in 1902 whereby it would evacuate Manchuria in three stages. Only the first of these, entailing the partial evacuation of the south, was actually concluded, albeit to a somewhat greater extent than called for.

Nicholas II's government was divided over what to do in Manchuria, and the tsar himself listened to the most hawkish counsels, becoming in the end the chief hawk himself. Relations with Japan were mishandled, with a change of mind about the agreement of 1898 that had seemed to offer the chance of a compromise. Knowing that they could not swallow Manchuria, the Russians nevertheless refused to give it up and even refused to accept that Korea should be part of Japan's sphere of influence. The situation was further complicated by the rising trouble inside Russia. Backward peasants overburdened with taxation and payments to the government for the land acquired at emancipation, workers suffering the unmitigated evils of capitalist exploitation, intelligentisia deprived of civil rights and political freedoms, and three Marxist revolutionary parties all seethed with discontent. To some Russian officials, such as Plehve, the minister of the interior, war with Japan offered a chance to rally the nation and escape revolution.

Japan obliged with a sudden attack on Port Arthur in January 1904 (exactly like the December 1941 attack on Pearl Harbour), and the Russians were defeated with heavy casualties in a war lasting nearly two years. The Chinese of Manchuria had not hated the Russians to the point that they were willing to make any special effort to help replace them by another conqueror, so they maintained a fairly consistent neutrality although suffering heavy casualties and devastation. Northern Manchuria however escaped damage and enjoyed great economic development through housing refugees from the south and catering for Russian military needs.

By the Peace of Portsmouth in 1906 Russian had to hand over all its property in Southern Manchuria, retaining only the CER. It also had to evacuate its army from Manchuria entirely, return to China various mines and telegraph lines, and consent to the opening of the North Manchurian towns to international settlement as treaty ports, and to the extension of the work of the Imperial Chinese Maritime Customs (ICMC) to Northern Manchuria. The net result of this was that Russian influence was to be restricted almost entirely to the CER, and diluted even there.

The defeat at the hands of Japan was the catalyst which set in motion the 1905 revolution in Russia. But owing to the complete isolation from each other of the middle-class, peasant and worker movements, the loyalty of the army and the strong financial backing of the French government, the tsar and his advisers were able to ride out this storm. The middle class was placated with the offer of a weak consultative Parliament, the peasants freed from the redemption dues, and the workers given the right to form local trades unions, after which concessions the worker and peasant movements were crushed by force.

Having weathered the revolution, St Petersburg accepted the loss of its position in Northern Manchuria very unwillingly. Long negotiations were held with the Chinese before the Russian army was finally with drawn in 1907. But with Russian weakness exposed, the Chinese were able to recover most of their rights in Northern Manchuria. At this eleventh hour the Qing dynasty embarked on a belated programme of reform and the whole Chinese nation became caught up in an enthusiasm for the regeneration of their country. Army reform, already well advanced, was pressed ahead. Chinese civilian governors were put in charge of the Manchurian provinces in place of the old Manchu generals, a national network of state schools was started, and finally representative assemblies were allowed in each province.

St Petersburg fought back in Northern Manchuria by trying to introduce self-government to the Russian settlements on the CER in an attempt to get the powers to recognise them as Russian property. But in a series of agreements between 1907 and 1910 the tsarist position on the CER was whittled down. The company's lands were recognised as part of the territory of China, CER mining and lumbering rights were reduced, Chinese troops allowed to enter the railway zone to pursue bandits, and the consuls of the various powers and the ICMC established themselves in Harbin. The Russian government framed its policies to encourage the economic development of its Far Eastern territories at the expense of the Russians on the CER and soon came to terms with its former enemy, Japan, in a series of agreements concluded in 1907, 1910 and 1912. These allotted Northern Manchuria and Outer Mongolia (where Russian interest and prestige were ever-growing) to St Petersburg's sphere of influence, and Southern Manchuria and Inner Mongolia to

Tokyo's. Russia and Japan combined diplomatically to exclude other powers from attempting to threaten their positions in these regions. Thus they obstructed the progress of the six-power consortium loans offered to China in 1910 for the industrial development of Manchuria.

In 1911 the outbreak of the Chinese revolution created an entirely new situation. The Manchu dynasty and the great gentry families of Peking intimately connected with it were toppled from power in a widespread movement triggered off by the efforts of a young Western-educated Chinese doctor, Sun Yatsen, and his small band of revolutionaries.

The old regime was destroyed, yet there was little support for the Western-style parliamentary government envisaged by Sun Yatsen. A republic was set up in China, but it was very weak. As no strong central government could be re-established, the country swiftly began to fall apart into regional groupings, in which the commanders of the new army units, in most cases men of humble origin, emerged as the strongest figures. These were the so-called warlords. In the south Sun Yatsen struggled to keep his liberal party alive, and in Peking the first president of the republic, Yuan Shikai, aimed to restore monarchy by himself founding a new Chinese dynasty, but died in 1916. The Chinese revolution seemed to be running into the sands, but despite the feebleness of the new China, the powers were at first too jealous of one another to make a move to dismember it. Russia along with the others recognised the republic.

But Russia was not long in taking some advantage of these new opportunities. With Russian backing the Outer Mongols declared their independence of China in 1912 and became a protectorate of Russia, although China bitterly resented this. As a sop to Chinese feeling, an agreement in 1913 and the Treaty of Kiakhta in 1915 recognised Outer Mongolia as still a part of China, but it was lip service only.

In the summer of 1913 the Russians brought pressure to bear with troops on the governor of Heilongjiang province in Northern Manchuria, forcing him to resign in favour of a more compliant individual. Until 1917 Russia maintained in Heilongjiang a rather slighter amount of control than exercised there during its military occupation in 1900–05. Its troops were generally confined to the CER zone. Kirin, the other Northern Manchurian province, managed to balance between the Russians and

Japanese and maintain a precarious independence of both.

In 1913 Russia also helped the Mongols of the Hurunbuir region of Northwest Manchuria to become partly independent of China under Russian protection, and in 1916 it obtained a concession from China to build another great railway linking the CER with the Russian town of Blagoveshchensk on the Siberian side of the Amur, but this was never made.

Apart from Manchuria and Mongolia Russia also enjoyed commercial and political influence in two areas of Xinjiang, around Kashgar in the south and Ili and Tarbagatai in the northwest. Its prestige in Kashgar had however become less than that of the British since the 1905 revolution and the Russian defeat by Japan.

Russia's entry into the First World War against Germany spelled the death-knell of the tsarist regime. So incompetent was the tsar's government that the country was soon subjected to all manner of economic dislocations, and the mobilisation of resources had to be taken over largely by voluntary effort through the local government organisations and a committee of the Duma. Yet the tsar still stubbornly refused to give any real political power to the Duma.

In the Far East, the Russian frontier troops and those who guarded the CER were drafted away to the front, leaving large stretches of the borders virtually unwatched and the CER tended by a poorly disciplined militia of middle-aged and very young men. Yet, cut off from its allies in Europe by the advancing German and Austro-Hungarian armies, Russia's only major supply line now lay through Vladivostok and the CER. Huge imports from the United States and Japan flowed along this route, and the CER zone itself enjoyed a hectic prosperity as a source of supplies for war-torn Russia. Russia fell increasingly into dependence on Japan for credits and armaments, so that by the time the last tsarist-Japanese treaty was signed in 1916, creating an alliance between the two countries, Tokyo had begun to make demands threatening Russia's position in Manchuria and its Far Eastern provinces. The hope of annexing Northern Manchuria, nurtured by the Russian government since 1910 at least, grew dimmer. Japan had already in 1915 issued the notorious 21 Demands against China, showing plainly that it wanted to reduce all China to its protectorate. The fall of the tsarist regime thus found Russia in a generally weakened position in Manchuria and

Kashgar, but with dominant influence over Outer Mongolia and strong influence in the Ili region.

Revolution broke out in Russia in March 1917. The tsar and his government had outworn everyone's patience, and in the end an outburst of strikes and demonstrations in Petrograd (as St Petersburg had been renamed), joined by the troops sent to suppress them, sufficed to topple the old regime. A Provisional government was formed, mainly of liberals, but with increasing socialist participation as the year went on. It introduced complete political liberty with autonomy for the minorities, but would not end the unpopular war nor quickly satisfy the demands of the peasants for more land and of the workers for better conditions. Leisurely preparations were made for democratic elections to a National Constituent Assembly. Thus there was an impatient shift of public opinion to the left, and rising anarchy. The authority of the government was challenged by the Soviets, a spontaneous democratic movement of popular councils which grew up all over the country, in villages and towns. Chaotic in organisation, the Soviets were easily dominated by members of three competing Marxist revolutionary parties. Of these the Bolsheviks, the most radical and tightly organised, grew in strength under the gifted leadership of their leader Lenin.

The China policy of the Provisional government belied its liberal domestic line, for it tried to maintain and increase the Russian hold wherever it existed. But, as disorder and disunity increased in Russia and a version of the revolution at home took place amongst the Russians of the CER zone, Russian influence in China rapidly collapsed. In the summer of 1917 all its power outside the CER zone had vanished The Mongols of Hurunbuir turned to Japan for support against China, and Zhang Zuolin, the rising warlord to Manchuria, installed one of his own supporters as governor of Heilongjiang. In Kashgar the British were dominant, and even in Ili Russia ceased to count politically.

But if Russia's position in China was falling to a low ebb, so was the authority of the Chinese themselves. The conservative warlord government now installed in Peking was unable to do much without the sanction of the allied governments. It watched the leftward swing in Russia with a disapproval strengthened by theirs.

9 1917-1943:

SOVIET RUSSIA AND DIVIDED CHINA

In the autumn of 1917 the peasants rose throughout European Russia and seized the estates of the landowners. Sentiment in the army and the towns swung towards the Bolsheviks, who had majorities in the Soviets of the important cities of European Russia by the end of October. The Provisional government was totally irresolute, commanding no loyal armed force. Lenin now judged the moment ripe for action, and pushed his hesitant colleagues into seizing power. On 7 November 1917 the Bolsheviks with a small force of soldiers and workers toppled the Provisional government, and proclaimed the world's first 'worker and peasant state'. Within weeks they had extended their control over central European Russia, the key heartland of the empire.

Lenin consolidated Bolshevik power by a mixture of reform and force—in theory the dictatorship of the proletariat, in practice the dictatorship of the Bolshevik party. Within months the capital had been moved back to Moscow, peace concluded with Germany, the liberal apparatus of the Provisional government period dismantled, and the country turned away from the Westernising tendency of the previous 220 years towards a new, more Eurasian path of authoritarian rule and state socialist development of the whole empire. Unable to prevent the elections to the Constituent Assembly, Lenin broke up the chamber which resulted from them, for it was dominated by the Social Revolutionaries, the mainly peasant-backed democratic Marxist party. Yet so great was the political apathy of most Russians that there was little reaction to this destruction of their new-found political liberty. The average peasant or worker Russian was more concerned with problems of survival, and many of the upper and middle class were in full flight abroad.

Soviet Russia became more Eurasian over the years in the sense that it was isolated politically and ideologically from the West, developing its own new centralised, bureaucratic Soviet institutions which in some ways seemed to hark back in spirit to the old Russia of the tsars before Alexander II, and even to Muscovy. At the same time, the rivalry with the capitalist world and the stress on popular welfare which was basic to the Bolshevik platform (even though second to state strengthening) led to much more interest in Asia and the Asian regions of the country. The minorities, who occupied large and important areas of the empire, had mostly been reconquered by 1922, and although the political system of the Soviet Union left the Russians dominant, it gradually provided the Asians with economic development, education and advancement, and an executive autonomy allowing them increasingly to run their own affairs under Moscow's supervision. (The impact on the more Europe-orientated Western minorities was less fortunate.)

All this was a general broad movement that gathered momentum over time. In the meanwhile, by summer 1918 the officers of the old Russian army (transformed by events into a slightly superior type of warlord) and scattered Social Revolutionary groups had started a civil war against the Bolsheviks with the half-hearted backing of small contingents of British, French and US troops. Japan precipitated the allied intervention in the Far East by seizing the chance to occupy the Russian Far Eastern provinces in the summer of 1918. China took a token part in the intervention. But the disunity and corruption of the White (anti-Bolshevik) Russians and the superior elan of the Red army led to Moscow's victory in the civil war by the end of 1920, and the evacuation of the allied expeditionary forces. The civil war was very bitter and rank with atrocities on both sides; it left Russia in rags, with industrial and agriculture output fallen to about half the level of 1914. To win the civil war, the Bolsheviks relied on a harsh system of total nationalisation and requisitioning known as War Communism.

Against this background of war and diplomatic isolation the Soviet government soon launched into a policy of seeking friendship and influence everywhere possible in divided China, for China remained a semi-vacuum from which hostile interests could threaten the security of Soviet Russia's long frontiers. In the hectic aftermath of the November revolution Lenin and Trotsky had urged the Bolshevik faction on the CER to seize the railway in the name of the workers' and peasants' government, regardless of the fact that it lay on Chinese soil. But the local Bolsheviks, relying on the undisciplined militia and lacking qualified personnel, were unable to do so. Instead, the wily tsarist manager of the railway, General Horvath, tried to talk them around with threats of intervention by the Peking government. He too failed, hampered by the mistrust of the liberals and other non-Bolshevik groups — and the Chinese decisively came into their own through a well-disciplined military occupation of Harbin. On 26 December 1917 they disarmed the pro-Bolshevik Russian militia, the first time in history that any group of Europeans, having reduced themselves to anarchy, had been brought under the control of Chinese.

Divided China might be, but it was a cardinal object of any Chinese regime however weak to resist encroachment of foreigners in so far as this was possible. The Chinese intervention was set in motion with the approval of the Western powers, but the latter had hoped to use it, as Horvath had tried to do, as a minatory gesture only. The actual seizure of military control over the CER by China exceeded their real wishes. Thereafter, Horvath ran a shaky anti-Bolshevik regime on the railway, always under a measure of Chinese restraint. He was unable to rebuild a significant armed force. Growing Japanese ambitions in the Far East finally prompted the war-weakened Britain and France and isolation-inclined United States to thwart Japan by establishing a joint control of the CER in 1919, the Interallied Technical Board.

This formed an umbrella beneath which in 1919 Chinese steamships started navigating the Amur, a right which the Russians had hitherto prevented but which was never lost to China again. Likewise in 1920 the strong Chinese governor of Heilungjiang managed to oust Horvath, who at the last became unpopular with the Russian workers in the railway zone. A new board of directors was appointed to the CER, partly Chinese and partly French; from 1920 to 1924 the line was run by Ostroumov, a very efficient White Russian manager, with French financial backing and some slight Chinese participation. In 1920 also Peking withdrew recognition from the tsarist minister to China (who had been hanging on at his post with allied support since the revolution), and cancelled the extra-territorial rights of Russians on Chinese soil. This place some 300 000, often destitute, Russian refugees from the revolutions at the mercy of the corrupt Chinese judicial system of the day.

The Bolshevik government had itself in 1918 renounced extra-territoriality and the Tsarist concessions except the CER, but tried vainly to regain hold of that and to get recognition from the Peking government. Even the so-called Karakhan Declaration of 1919, appearing to renounce the CER, did not win round the Chinese and was soon reneged upon. Finally the Soviet envoy Yurin was received in the Chinese capital for negotiations in 1920. For nearly four years he and three later envoys (Paikes, Joffe and Karakhan) strove to achieve Moscow's desired ends. In this they were hindered by rising Soviet demands and Soviet successes in Mongolia, which had fallen back under Chinese influence with unpleasant results in 1917 and was later occupied by a White Russian warlord, but which turned again to Moscow in 1921. June of that year saw a Soviet army occupy the country with a measure of support from the people, to the annoyance of China.

The general turn of world events, however, aided the Soviet cause. After Bolshevik victory in the civil war, Lenin stilled the discontent in his ruined, starving country by US famine relief and the New Economic Policy, which restored small-scale industry and retail trade to private hands and was more lenient to the peasants. Between 1921 and 1927 conditions in Russia improved steadily and output returned to the 1914 level. In 1921 trade recommenced between most European countries and the Soviet Union, which also normalised diplomatic relations with its bordering European and Middle Eastern states. In April 1922 the Soviet Union and Germany concluded the Treaty of Rapallo, inaugurating normal diplomatic relations between them together with commercial and secret military collaboration. Tokyo, with which Moscow was negotiating at the same time as with Peking, gradually abandoned its Siberian and Manchurian adventure in the face of popular opposition in Japan. By 1919 public opinion in China had also rallied against Japanese demands. At the same time the United States had turned to isolation, and Britain and France were too much weakened ever again to exert much authority in Northeast Asia. Japan withdrew its last troops from the Maritime Province in November 1922, and the Interallied Technical Board was promptly wound up. Moscow's power flooded back to the Pacific shores, and the CER was almost within its grasp.

Still the Peking government stalled, but Britain's recognition of the Soviet Union in February 1924, an improving climate in the Tokyo–Moscow negotiations and Moscow's new friendship with Sun Yatsen (of which more in a moment) finally induced China's warlord government to sign the 1924 Treaty of Friendship with the Soviet Union in May of the same year. Full diplomatic relations were commenced, and the White Russian share of the CER was handed over to Moscow. A separate agreement confirming this was also concluded with Zhang Zuolin's Japanese-protected warlord government in Mukden. But conferences on border problems which followed ran into a dead end, for neither the Peking nor Moscow government was in a position to negotiate from the strength it would have wished on this vital issue.

By 1919 China was again in one of the vast spasms of the revolution which was propelling it out of the Middle Ages into the modern world. From the end of the nineteenth century the Chinese intelligentsia had been experiencing a mounting wave of intellectual curiosity and learning from abroad, comparable to the enlightenment of late-eighteenth-century Russia, and this gathered great momentum after the First World War. The Russian revolution prompted interest in Marxism, so that by 1920 the first small Marxist groups were formed under Chen Duxiu and Li Dazhao. In the spring of that year Voitinskii, an emissary of the Comintern (which had been set up in Moscow in January 1919 under Lenin's control), visited Chen and Li. With the close oversight of the Russians the Chinese Communist Party (CCP) was then established, holding its first conference in July 1921.

A general Communist strategy for Asia was laid down by Lenin at the Second Congress of the Comintern in November 1920. This provided that the infant Communist parties, as they arose, should ally with the bourgeois nationalist parties of their countries with the aim of over-throwing foreign rule or foreign influence and carrying out a bourgeois democratic revolution. Socialist revolutions should follow only after some considerable interval, when capitalism should have developed sufficiently to produce a large working class. This strategy of two-stage revolution contrasted with the virtual one-stage revolution which had taken place in Russia itself, where the Bolshevik revolution had followed within eight months of the bourgeois one with a prematurity that Lenin had begun exhaustedly to realise before stricken by his last illness late in 1922.

Meanwhile in South China Sun Yatsen was facing manifold problems in his attempt to lead his country into welfare democracy, in face of warlord intrigues and the incomprehension of the masses. His party attracted support from different social groups and classes, but its leaders were mostly landowners, although Sun himself was a man of quite humble origin educated abroad. In spring 1920 he appealed to all the powers for economic aid. The West and Japan were not ready to give him a fraction of what he wanted, so he turned an increasingly receptive ear to Moscow, which began to court him through visits from a succession of envoys. Finally he signed an agreement with the Soviet representative Joffe in January 1923, accepting Soviet military aid and advice on the understanding that Soviet interest in China was confined to the promotion of national unity and defence. It was a relatively short step further for the Russians to push Sun and the CCP into a United Front, announced publicly in January 1924.

Lenin's death on 21 January 1924 left Stalin the strongest man in Moscow. He had become the general secretary of the Soviet Communist Party in April 1922, and now had a considerable hold over the whole administration, despite challenge from Trotsky and his followers. Stalin insisted on maintaining the Chinese United Front but Trotsky, when he began to play a role in China policy from 1925, urged its end and the fostering of peasant revolution with rural soviets. Neither Stalin nor Trotsky had any deep commitment to China, their attention being mainly fixed on the Russian situation to which, for them, China was an appendage. But Stalin at least was well informed about Chinese realities by the Soviet advisers with Sun Yatsen.

In these years the Soviet Union was at a crossroads, for what was at stake was not only whether Stalin or Trotsky was to rule, but the very future of the regime. Powerful forces — the private businessmen and all the peasants — were still outside the control of the Communist Party. Stalin's policy of subordinating everything to building up a strong, socialist Russia contrasted with Trotsky's of promoting world revolution to assist the progress of the revolution at home. There were also important controversies involving many of the ruling group as to whether priority should be given to agricultural or industrial development, and as to whether economic autarky or close integration with Europe through trade should be sought.

The First United Front in China accomplished a certain amount for both the CCP and Guomindang (more widely known in Western usage as Kuo-min-tang—KMT). Soviet aid to the former, running at US$3000 a month in mid-1921, was curtailed later, but the party increased in numbers from 1000 in 1924 to 58 000 in March 1927, and strengthened its organisation. The KMT acquired from its Soviet advisers the political structure which it retains to this day in Taiwan. The Soviet government also contributed funds and personnel for the establishment of the Whampoa Military Academy, and consignments of arms, and helped in the formation of an effective KMT army and in bringing all of Guangdong province under Sun's control. In no sense, however, did Sun become a Russian puppet; he was careful to keep lines open to Japan, and towards the end of his life might have been contemplating a move against the Chinese Communists, if not against 60-odd Soviet advisers who had been sent to South China. For its part Moscow tried to develop other options too; between 1925 and 1927 military aid on a scale similar to that given to the KMT was also supplied to the so-called 'Christian' warlord Feng Yuxiang in North China.

With the death of Sun Yatsen in March 1925 anti-Communist leaders came to the fore in the KMT. Jiang Kaishek, who emerged as the strongest, started to crack down on the Communists and the Soviet advisers from 20 March 1926 when he dismissed a number of both from important posts in Canton on the pretext of a Communist plot to kidnap him—the Zhongshan incident. Despite opposition from Trotsky, Stalin had the remaining advisers and the Chinese Communists turn the other cheek and aid the KMT army in its northern expedition to reunify the whole of China, which Jiang started in June 1926. Early in 1927 the KMT split in two, with Jiang setting up his government in Jiangxi. The Communists remained in alliance with the leftist KMT, which established its seat at Wuhan on the Yangzi. There was a rising tide of peasant unrest in Central China, but Stalin ordered an equivocal policy towards it. The peasants must not be given free rein, for the most important thing in his eyes was to hold on to the alliance with the landowner leaders of the Wuhan government. Even when Jiang took the lower Yangzi cities of Shanghai and Nanking in March 1927, and massacred large numbers of city Chinese Communists in April,

Stalin stuck to the United Front, issuing more of the contradictory orders to hunt with the leftist KMT and run with the peasant movement at the same time. Matters were not helped when Feng Yuxiang came to terms with Jiang Kaishek.

Finally the position of the Soviet advisers in Wuhan became so untenable that the Indian Comintern agent M.N. Roy deliberately 'leaked' one of Stalin's telegrams to the Wuhan leader Wang Chingwei. In July 1927 the Communists both Chinese and Russian were expelled from Wuhan and Stalin's China policy was thrown into disarray. This was not fatal to him, since he had already got the better of Trotsky, who had been dismissed as commissar of war in 1925 and evicted from the Central Committee of the Communist Party at the end of 1926. In December 1927 Trotsky was expelled from the party itself and exiled, leaving Stalin supreme except for the residual influence of the weaker Bukharin. Stalin now proceeded to a programme of rapid industrialisation through the five year plans and the forced collectivisation of the small peasant farms, backed by a reign of terror imposed on both the Soviet people and the party by the secret police through whom he virtually ruled. Education and welfare systems were also expanded.

For good and for evil, Stalin transformed the Soviet Union. His legacy to the CCP through the United Front was a similarly mixed one. The blows dealt by Jiang and Wuhan to the CCP were very severe, yet it is hard to see how it could have survived its infant years without some form of United Front. For the present Stalin tried to save face in China by making a scape-goat of the first secretary of the Chinese party, Chen Duxiu, and by announcing that the Chinese revolution was now rising to a high tide, thus justifying a gradual transfer to a more Trotsky-style of policy. He selected as the new first secretary a Moscow-trained man named Chiu Chiobai, to carry out a new strategy of rural risings leading to the capture of key towns.

Chiu was the first of a series of Russian-educated Chinese who emerged from the two universities established in Moscow for foreigners: the Communist University for the Toilers of the East, founded in 1921 and many years later revived as the Patrice Lumumba, and the short-lived Sun Yatsen University for the Toilers of China (1925–30). A whole generation of Chinese leaders, both KMT and CCP, attended one or other of these institutions, including both Jiang Jingguo, the present ruler of

Taiwan, and Deng Xiaoping, the present leader of China. But these universities gave mixed results for the Soviet Union. Only a small minority of students appear to have been loyal to Stalin, and a number actually became clandestine followers of Trotsky. Most remained Chinese patriots first and foremost.

For the next few years relations between the KMT and the Soviet Union were bad. Jiang Kaishek turned to the Weimar Republic of Germany for advisers — Weimar incidentally still being on good terms with Moscow. By December 1927 he had closed down the Soviet consulates in his area. Zhang Zuolin did not yet touch those in Manchuria, for he hesitated to affront Moscow too much, although since spring 1925 he had been trying to overthrow the Soviet hold on the CER. At the start in 1924 the Soviets had dominated the line as much as ever the White Russians had done, but were making concession on concession. When they agreed in October 1927 to hand over 50 per cent of the profits to the Chinese members of the CER board, these became more willing partners in the enterprise and a wedge was driven betwen them and Zhang Zuolin. But Zhang's aims were continued by his son, Xueliang, after the father was assassinated by the Japanese in 1928. Jiang Kaishek gave his backing to the venture when he completed the loose unification of China after taking Peking in that same year, giving the title of National government to his regime. In face of the worsening situation Moscow broke off diplomatic ties with Nationalist China in April 1929, but the latter did not follow suit until July.

The seizure of the CER by the Mukden government with the blessing of the Nationalist government followed shortly after, the Chinese members of the board having co-operated at a late stage. The Chinese were unable to staff the line entirely with their own people, but merely turned the tables on the Russians, assuming the master role and replacing Soviet personnel with White Russians — of whom a good many had continued to be employed since 1924.

Stalin reacted with great skill. A war of nerves was carried out on the Manchurian frontiers by the Soviet Red army for several months. Carefully planned skirmishes and firing at unexpected points, coupled with the release of alarming rumours, produced a tense state in Zhang Xueliang's troops. Finally in November Stalin had his forces briefly invade Manchuria. After routing the less disciplined Chinese warlord soldiers, the Red army advanced a short distance and then withdrew in perfect order, having harmed nobody but unfortunate anti-Soviet White Russians in its path, who were removed to concentration camps in Siberia. Atrocities did apparently take place in Northwest Manchuria when Soviet forces raided the Cossack refugee settlements there.

Negotiations were soon opened between the Soviet Union and a representative of both the Mukden and Nanking governments, and the Soviet position on the CER was restored by the Khabarovsk Protocol of 22 December 1929. For the next eighteen months Soviet economic and political influence in Northern Manchuria increased rapidly, so that by March 1931 it seemed to the British consul in Harbin that the region was going to become a Soviet buffer state like Outer Mongolia. The relative immunity of the Soviet Union from the Great Depression then affecting the capitalist world explained this as much as the impressive Soviet record in the war of 1929.

After 1929 the Chinese consulates in the Soviet Union were not re-opened, and Stalin by one means or another obtained the removal of most of the remainder of the one-time 300 000 or more Chinese in the Union. Many had already left when their businesses were closed at the end of the New Economic Policy, others were now deported or sent to concentration camps. Some few however did remain and become Soviet Chinese.

Soviet influence was waxing in Xinjiang too at this time. After the 1919 revolution it had faded to a low ebb, thereafter slowly recovering. As it did so, the semi-independent governor of the province from 1912 to 1928, Yang Zengxin, balanced between Britain and Moscow, allowing the former to continue its zone of influence around Kashgar in the south, adjoining British India, whilst the Russians enjoyed a similar one in the Ili area. But by 1924 Yang had to agree to a treaty with Moscow permitting Soviet consulates to be opened in Xinjiang in return for some of his own in Soviet territory. (These were closed with the others in 1929.) Yang's assassination in 1928 was followed by the rule of the warlord Jin Shuren, who cultivated ties with Weimar Germany as the Nationalist government was then doing, but alienated the Muslims of Xinjiang by abolishing their privileges and increasing corruption and taxation. In October 1931 he was obliged to make an agreement with the Soviet Union for assistance against the Muslim rebellion led by Ma Zhongying. In return he had to allow Moscow free trade, political representatives in five more places and financial offices in four key towns.

Elsewhere in the Far East Soviet prestige sagged. Between 1919 and 1931 Moscow's relations with Tokyo, which had enjoyed a brief phase of mild warmth since the 1925 treaty between them, began to deteriorate again. Moscow and Nanking remained on poor terms. A conference on the sale of the CER to the Nationalists was dragged out in Moscow between October 1930 and the late summer of 1931, without bridging the large gaps between the demands of each side. Moscow's main lever in China proper was perforce the CCP, but its hold over this began to weaken in this period. The Comintern was represented with it by just two European advisers from July 1927 to 1929, thereafter for the next fourteen years or so only by one (none was an ethnic Russian). This reflected not only the dangerous clandestine conditions in which the CCP now operated, but also probably Stalin's preference for working with governments and winning concrete benefits from borderland penetration.

Chiu Chiobai made consciencious efforts to execute the new Comintern line of fighting from the countryside into the towns. Three risings took place in South-Central China in 1927, only one of which possibly originated from Stalin's orders, although he approved all. All failed, but the one maybe ordered from Moscow, the Autumn Harvest Uprising, marked the start of Mao Zedong's independent career as a Communist leader, for after it he removed with his small band of followers to the Jiangxi mountains and began to evolve his own ideas. In February 1928 Chiu Chiobai in turn was made a scapegoat, but not heavily discredited. He was replaced by a new Moscow-appointed Central Committee of the CCP in July, under the leadership of Li Lisan. Li was supposed to continue with rural revolution, building up a Communist army but linking all military action in the country-side with risings in the towns. Yet in face of the growing independence of Mao in the mountains of Jiangxi and the difficulty of other rural action he was moved to launch hopeless risings in the towns alone in defiance of Stalin's orders.

In the spring of 1930 Stalin sent to the CCP the 'Returned Students' or '28 Bolsheviks', a batch of young Chinese from the Moscow universities of whom Chen Shaoyu, alias Wang Ming, became best known. Li Lisan was brought to trial and Wang and his companions were installed as leaders of the CCP by Pavel Mif, the Comintern representative, in January 1931. They had orders to supervise the affairs of the Communists in Jiangxi, and from April 1931 began to move there from their secret Shanghai headquarters. Finally all were driven by Nationalist persecution to do so. In the so-called Jiangxi Soviet between 1931 and autumn 1934 three groups co-operated and competed for leadership: the pro-Comintern Returned Students, certain independent-minded veterans like Zhang Guotao, and Mao and his associates. At first the Returned Students met with success, which culminated at the Second National Soviet Congress of the CCP in January–February 1934. But contact with Moscow was far slighter now, and the Chinese Communists were harassed by the Nationalist forces.

Then Moscow's prospects in Manchuria crumbled in 1931. Economic collapse faced this area in the wake of the Great Depression, from the effects of which Soviet trade alone could not save it, and the Mukden incident of 18 September marked the start of the Japanese armed takeover of Manchuria. The Japanese army entered Harbin on 5 February 1932, and the puppet state of Manzhuguo was established in March. For this reason the Nationalists and the Soviet Union recommenced diplomatic ties in December of that year, but stayed cool to one another.

In Manchuria the Soviet-dominated CER, with subordinate Chinese participation, existed under conditions of extreme stress with the Japanese, forced to make large payments to Manzhuguo officials and under constant attack from bandits in Japanese pay. Stalin managed to sell the CER to Japan in 1935 for 140 million yen, having come to an agreement over navigation on the border rivers with the Manzhuguo government in 1934, but relations remained very uneasy with many frontier clashes. After 1935 a few consulates were the sole residue of Soviet influence in Manchuria.

Meanwhile the CCP was under mounting military pressure from the KMT and was finally driven to escape annihilation by the heroic Long March of 6000 odd miles into the mountains of West China and back round to Shanxi province in the north between the autumn of 1934 and the spring of 1936. Not far from the borders of Inner Mongolia a new Communist stronghold was established at Yenan, amongst the loess-covered mountains, far from the centres of Nationalist strength. During the Long March the struggle for power continued. At the Cunyi conference of the CCP in Guizhou in January 1935 a new leadership emerged, with Mao the most dominant as chairman of the military affairs committee. But Zhang Guotao and the Comintern faction were still much to be reckoned with, Zhang being on the Central Committee and a Comintern man being general secretary of the party.

Hitler's coming to power in Germany in 1933 added Western dangers to those already facing the Soviet Union in the East. It also brought recognition at last from the United States, and entry to the League of Nations in 1934. But attempts to come to some definite understanding with the Western powers never bore much fruit. Neither the democracies nor Moscow trusted one another, though each wanted to prevent the other from allying with Hitler against themselves. A new policy of United Front with any party willing to resist Fascism was ordered on the Communist parties by the seventh Comintern congress in July–August 1935.

Wang Ming, as CCP representative at this, spoke for Stalin when he called for a drastic re-orientation of the party's policy and a government of national defence in China. But it took over two years to realise a semblance of this aim. The Chinese Communists, then still on the march, agreed in December only to a loose United Front, directed as much against the Nationalists as against the Japanese, and the Nationalists were far less inclined to come round. Germany, Italy and Japan signed the Anti-Comintern Pact in November 1936, and Jiang seemed to be moving towards association with this until his spectacular kidnapping by Zhang Xueliang at Sian on 12 December. Zhang held Jiang captive until he agreed to a United Front to resist Japan; in March Jiang announced stiff terms for this, but the Chinese Communists did not agree.

Then on 7 July came the Marco Polo bridge incident, plainly revealing the will of Japan to subdue China. Jiang stood up to the Japanese and concluded a non-aggression pact with the Soviet Union on 31 August. The CCP gave in the next day, having no alternative. The second United Front was announced on 1 September — a United Front from Without, simply a tactical alliance and much less than Moscow wanted.

The Nationalists were the party favoured by the Soviet government in this grouping. Several hundred million US dollars in loans and credits were supplied to it by Moscow, together with a substantial number of warplanes. A large Soviet military mission was set up in China, acting as technical consultants, and some 200 or more Soviet pilots flew on active service against the

Japanese. Amongst the officers in the military mission were such later renowned figures as Zhukov, the conqueror of Berlin in the Second World War, and Chuikov, the defender of Stalingrad. No other country gave China any assistance against Japan at this time.

Soviet military aid to the Nationalists was channelled through Xinjiang, which by this time had become virtually a Soviet buffer state. During the Ma Zhongying Muslim rebellion against the warlord Jin Shuren, Moscow had supported both sides to some extent. Despite a vain attempt by Jiang Kaishek to re-assert the central government's interest in the province in 1933, Jin Shuren was killed and succeeded by the Soviet-backed Sheng Shicai in April of that year. Already 90 per cent of the trade of Xinjiang was with the Soviet Union. Through Sheng, Moscow now acquired control of its oil and other mineral wealth, and in return supplied aid for modernisation, on the Soviet model, but without socialism. A series of five year plans was launched in 1936, a Cyrillic alphabet introduced for the Muslim nationalities who formed the majority of the population, medical facilities improved, and so on. Some Soviet troops were stationed in the Ili region.

By the spring of 1941 Stalin had extricated the Soviet Union, as he believed, from the dangers pressing upon it. The Japanese stepped up their probing attacks on the Soviet Manchurian and Outer Mongolian borders in the late 1930s, culminating in two large pitched battles, at Khasan Nor in July 1938 and at Nomonhan on the Khalkin River on 30 August 1939. Both these places were on the border with Outer Mongolia, and resulted in sound defeats for the Japanese at the hands of Soviet and Mongol troops. This was not the least of the factors which decided Japan to turn south against the Asian empires of the Western powers, rather than to invade Siberia again, as had seemed on the cards since 1932. After Nomonhan, Soviet-Japanese relations improved somewhat.

Seven days before Nomonhan, on 23 August 1939, Stalin had concluded a non-aggression pact with Hitler, in accordance with which the Soviet Union partitioned Poland with Germany in September and in the summer of 1940 occupied Bessarabia and the Baltic states, which had won their freedom from Russia after the First World War. On 3 April 1941 the safety of the Soviet Union was reinforced by the Soviet-Japanese neutrality pact, which unlike the agreement with Hitler really worked, as Japan was at war with the United States by the end of the year. The Hitler pact won the Russians less than two years valuable respite before they had to face the full force of the German army on 22 June 1941. Stalin's faith in Hitler had been completely misplaced, but his economic achievements, especially the creation of the Urals industrial base, enabled the Soviet Union to withstand the German invasion.

Meanwhile the Japanese had gone on attacking China, with the brunt of the intermittent fighting being borne by the Nationalists. The Chinese Communists received no Soviet aid, and followed their own interests. Immediately after the inauguration of the United Front, in October 1937, Mao Zedong ousted Zhang Guotao and the Comintern endorsed his leadership, perhaps to put him off his guard. In December Wang Ming was smuggled to Yenan from Moscow with orders to assume leadership in place of Mao and make the CCP devote its major efforts to the anti-Japanese struggle instead of fighting the KMT. But after transient successes, Wang was defeated by Mao at the Sixth Party Plenum in October 1938, and later further discredited in 1942 when the Eighth Route army, commanded by his followers, was badly beaten in battle with the Japanese. Mao became supreme in 1942 and Wang Ming lost all influence. In 1943 he had to be taken back to Moscow by the Russians. (According to a Soviet source, Mao was trying to poison him by having him dosed with rotten calomel lotion for some illness).

Co-operation between the Nationalists and the Communists against the Japanese practically ended with January 1941. Mao perfected his own theories and his own strategies for winning power in China, harnessing the loyalties of the peasants through land reform and attention to their welfare, and regenerating their spirit through a strict Marxist-cum-peasant code of social equality, morality and better treatment of women. Mao continued, however, to pay lip service to Soviet supremacy in the Communist world. Until late summer in 1939 the lone European Comintern representative at Yenan was the German Otto Braun, who had been with the Chinese Communists since before the Long March and throughout it. He was replaced by various new Soviet representatives flown in from Russia in the early 1940s, in the guise of pressmen and so on, but like Braun they were there as observers only and had no hold over Mao or his policies.

Soviet aid to the Nationalists was reduced from 1940 and it ceased altogether after the German attack on Russia. Soon after that, in August 1941, Jiang Kaishek came to some understanding with Sheng Shicai, and in October 1942, when the Soviet Red army was facing the Wehrmacht in the most crucial battle of the war at Stalingrad, Sheng requested that all Soviet military and technical personnel leave Xinjiang. In January 1943 Nationalist officials took over the province. Stalin rejected pleas from Nanking to continue economic and technical aid for it, gradually removing all his men by October 1943 (though a joint Soviet-Xinjiang airline remained in existence). He had now switched from a policy of upholding a Chinese warlord to one of very cautiously playing off the Turkic peoples of Xinjiang against their Chinese rulers. Relations between Moscow and the Nationalists deteriorated, but the Soviet embassy and military mission remained with them in their wartime capital of Chongqing through 1943.

As in 1917, Russian power in China in 1942 and 1943 was at a low ebb, and the national spirit of the Chinese was asserting itself across their political spectrum. Yet, as the tide of war turned in favour of the Soviet Union and the Soviet army began to battle its way back westwards towards Germany, the straws were in the wind for another major change in Sino-Soviet relations.

10   1943-1950:

ORIGINS OF THE SINO-SOVIET ALLIANCE

The last really important battle of the Russo-German war took place in the Kursk-Orel section of the front in July–August 1943. After this the Germans were slowly pressed back, and the victory of the Soviet Union was obviously only a matter of time. The major aim of both Stalin and Roosevelt at that time was a foreign policy partnership between their two countries in the post-war world. Stalin clearly mistrusted Mao, over whose regime he had even less control than over Jiang's, and plainly he hoped to play off the CCP and KMT, advancing Soviet interests in the borderlands and keeping China somewhat weak and divided but avoiding an all-out civil war. Roosevelt envisaged a China at peace under Jiang, but was much more afraid of the remaining Japanese war potential than Stalin appears to have been and ready to pay heavily for Soviet entry into the war with Japan. The Nationalist and Communist Chinese were long since embarked on a struggle to the death: efforts at compromise between them were merely tactical, for each knew that in the last resort a united China could only contain one of them. Jiang Kaishek opposed the Russians, looking for salvation to America, despite the existence of a weak pro-Soviet wing in the KMT, but the Chinese Communists tried to keep their foreign policy options as open as possible.

Stalin early tried to exact the highest price as a reward for his joining the war on Japan. At the First Cairo Conference in November 1943, Roosevelt extracted from Jiang an undertaking to bring the Chinese Communists into his government and promised a joint Nationalist-American occupation of Manchuria to keep the Soviet Union out. Yet within a few days, at the Teheran Conference of 27 November–2 December, Stalin had induced Roosevelt to promise him a warm-water port in Manchuria.

From mid-1943, partly as a result of the Xinjiang affair, the Soviet government gradually began to assume a somewhat more intimidating posture towards the Nationalists and in 1944 withdrew its military mission from Chongqing, although its ambassador continued there. As a corollary, Stalin began to make some small gestures of amity towards Yenan, but indicated to visiting Americans that he had no great respect for the Chinese Communists as Communists nor faith in their chances of winning in China. Mao for his part held unsuccessful talks with the Nationalists in May and June 1944, and thereafter welcomed a US military mission to Yenan. He made a genuine, bold bid for US support, signing a five-point agreement for a coalition government in China with the US representative Patrick Hurley in November 1944.

At the Yalta Conference of 4–11 February 1945, however, the failing Roosevelt conceded to Stalin in private that the Soviet Union should have South Sakhalin, the Kurile Islands, the *status quo* in Mongolia and control of the Manchurian ports and railways in return for coming into the war with Japan. Stalin now had a fresh inducement to keep on good terms with the Nationalists, since only they, as the recognised government of China, were in a position to deliver the Manchurian booty contractually. The United States also relied on Jiang to pay this price to get the Soviet army into the field against the excessively dreaded, but actually now much weakened, Japanese.

Roosevelt's death on 12 April made no immediate difference, for President Truman committed himself to maintaining all the late president's pledges. Germany surrendered on 7 May, and the Russians and Americans prepared to close in on Japan.

In Yenan the Seventh Congress of the CCP in April–June 1945 excluded all the former pro-Soviet faction from the Politburo, confirming the complete ascendancy of Mao and the nullification of the Russian's twenty-year struggle to build an obedient Chinese party—a point certainly not lost on Stalin.

There was no significant shift in the basic positions of the four parties till late in the year. The Yalta decision was reconfirmed in talks in Moscow between Truman's envoy Harry Hopkins and Stalin between 26 May and 2 June. After this, on Stalin's insistence, Jiang Kaishek was officially informed of the concessions China would have to make. He at once tried to get the United States to be a party to the Manchurian settlement, but

Washington refused. At the end of June Jiang's Foreign Minister, T.V. Soong, arrived in Moscow for the negotiations. From the time of the Potsdam Conference in July, however, Truman began to regret the US decision on Manchuria and tried to return to something near the Cairo I position, but it was too late. Stalin made some worthless verbal concessions and told Truman he would be ready to attack the Japanese in Manchuria by mid-August.

On 6 August without warning to Stalin the United States dropped the atomic bomb on Hiroshima, and on 8 August Stalin too declared war on Japan, jumping the gun on Truman as the latter had done to him. The following day the Soviet army invaded Manchuria with 1.5 million men. Both Soviet and US troops raced for the Manchurian and Korean ports, but the Soviet army, far better organised on the mainland, quickly occupied Manchuria and North Korea. The United States managed to get South Korea, but concentrated mainly on seizing control of Japan, from which it succeeded in totally excluding the Soviet Union.

Japan surrendered on 14 August and on the same day the Nationalist Chinese finally signed a treaty in Moscow giving the Russians nominally half-control of the Manchurian railways and the two ports of Lushun and Dalienwan (Port Arthur and Dal'ny/ Darien). Since there was no kind of Nationalist Chinese administration or military force in Manchuria, real control rested with the Soviet Union and its powerful army.

Stalin's main aims were now to hold on to the territories occupied by the Soviet army and at the same time to secure peace for his war-ravaged country. As American ill-will toward the former goal became more evident, he countered with an increasingly fierce display of hostility designed to mask Soviet weakness from the largely intact power of the United States. In Manchuria he followed at first a distinct divide-and-rule line, also designed to promote the extension of Soviet influence and the establishment of a coalition government in China. The CER was hastily converted to broad gauge, like the Soviet railways, and Soviet consuls assumed control over the White Russian community. The letter of the treaty of 14 August was followed on the railways, where Nationalist officials were allowed to assume posts, but Nationalist troops were prevented from entering Manchuria at the beginning, when they tried to do so with US help. In Lushun and

Dalienwan, however, Chinese Communists—some local, some from Yenan—were mainly appointed to work under the Soviet military regime, with a few figurehead Nationalists for a while.

Perhaps without consultation with the Russians and even against their wishes, Mao poured his troops into Manchuria from August onwards. On 28 August, in response to pressure from the Americans, he went to Chongqing for negotiations with Jiang. Stalin apparently backed this too, but left the Americans to do the urging. Five meetings were held over 41 days with no real agreement reached, and Mao's initiative was criticised by some of the other Chinese Communists. In mid-September Stalin sent representatives to Yenan, informing Mao (according to two sources) that he would support a Manchurian people's movement, and asking that the Chinese Communist Eighth Route army be withdrawn from Manchuria whilst the Soviet army was there. Mao's response to this was to redouble his efforts to establish a strong presence there. With or without Soviet consent Chinese Communist committees were established in Harbin, Mukden and other places.

The Soviet invasion army of 1945 was no longer the admirably disciplined revolutionary force of 1929. Brutalised by the war and its attendant horrors, the Soviet soldiers were allowed a period of licence to do what they liked with the enemy in Manchuria, as they had been in the ex-Nazi allies, Rumania and Hungary, and in Austria and Germany. The resultant orgies of raping and looting took the commanders a long time to bring under control again, and in Manchuria were directed against Chinese as well as Japanese, probably because the troops found it hard to distinguish them.

Stalin appeared bent on establishing Soviet influence in Manchuria. On 12 October talks began in Mukden between his representatives and the Nationalists on the fate of Manchurian industry, over which Stalin demanded joint control in return for allowing the Nationalist army's return to the area. These demands were resisted by the Nationalists to the end, with the Russians from time to time encouraging them to yield by facilitating the entry of batches of their troops to the region. On 27 November they even signed an agreement permitting the return of the northeast to Nationalist administration, but in fact the Chinese Communists were already too well entrenched in the northern parts of the country for Jiang Kaishek's men to be able to take over much more than the main trunk-line from Harbin to somewhere north of the Russian-controlled military zone in the Liaodong peninsula. Nationalist administrations were set up in Harbin, Changchun and Mukden, co-existing with the Communist in Harbin.

The agreement of 27 November prompted Mao to make another move towards the United States, welcoming the Marshall mission. General Marshall, the last and best US China conciliator, did succeed in patching up a cease-fire agreement between the Nationalists and Communists between 22 December and 11 March, and US forces were used to enforce the cease-fire arrangements in the Communists' favour in Manchuria in January.

Yet by the middle of December the Chinese Communists seem to have aligned themselves closely with Moscow, although Mao maintained some conciliatory gestures towards the United States or at least to Truman personally until May 1946. It is not yet possible to say exactly how this change came about. Despite the Marshall mission the United States went on aiding the Nationalists, whom Truman recognised as the only legal government of China in his speech of 15 December. During the Foreign Ministers' Conference in Moscow from 16 to 26 December the Soviet press sided with the 'democratic' elements in China and attacked the United States for keeping its marines there. It may be that Mao was anxious to prevent a Soviet–Nationalist deal to his disadvantage—Jiang's son Jingguo went to Moscow on 25 December and Stalin invited Jiang himself to meet him—or the fostering of separatist movements by the Russians. There was little evidence of any serious pro-Russian tendency amongst the Chinese Communists now, or of any hopeful Russian move to seek for such again. But an Eastern Mongolian autonomous government was established in Hurunbuir on 16 January 1946 with Soviet backing, and it looks as if Stalin was moving to detach this region from China, as its Mongol inhabitants had long wanted to join Outer Mongolia. Mao gained control of Western Inner Mongolia. In any case multiple political, economic and social factors seemed to draw the Communists towards Moscow and the Nationalists towards Washington, as the two great powers themselves drifted into more and more hostile attitudes towards each other.

Stalin for his part kept some lines open to the Nationalists through thick and thin. In May he extended another invitation to Jiang to visit him in Moscow, but this like the first was declined, and violent resentment at the conduct of the Soviet troops in Manchuria was deliberately fanned in the Nationalist-held areas. Faced with dubious prospects and an over-extended military position Stalin now withdrew his army from Manchuria between 7 March and 3 May 1946, also evacuating his forces from Northern Iran at about the same time. Henceforth he was to concentrate on Eastern Europe and Korea.

Upon the departure of the Soviet army, the civil war flared up in Manchuria. Chinese Communists moved into some towns, such as Sipinghai and Harbin, but the Nationalist forces very soon counter-attacked, seizing Mukden, winning a pitched battle over the Communists at Sipinghai, taking Changchun and moving on Harbin. Jiang Kaishek began to demand that Nationalist forces be stationed on the CER, but Marshall managed to secure a truce in Manchuria from 6 June 1946.

In those areas where the Nationalists remained in control, or where they took over, the Soviet railway administration was dismissed and Soviet railway personnel were subjected to various persecutions and indignities, according to Soviet sources. Within a short time Soviet civilian personnel outside the Communist-held areas and the Lushun base were withdrawn, but White Russians continued to be employed on the railways by the Nationalists.

The Soviet Russians gave economic and technical assistance to the Communist-held areas of Manchuria, and both they and the Chinese Communists tried assiduously to behave well to one another. As a result the harm done to the Russian image by the Soviet troops was gradually undone, and by 1948 Chinese-Soviet relations in Manchuria were considered by both the US consul in Mukden and White Russian observers to be much improved. They continued good until the late 1950s at least. Soviet military aid to the Chinese Communists however, was limited to substantial transfers of captured Japanese war material.

Within a year of Marshall's truce the civil war resumed again. During campaigns from May 1947 to March 1948 the Communists overran all central Manchuria, isolating the Nationalists in Changchun and Mukden. A renewed onslaught on these positions in September 1948 led to the complete Communist conquest of Manchuria by 5 November. Already in 1947 Stalin had probably put into cold storage much of whatever direct ambition he may have had in Northeast China. From the beginning of that year the CER was progressively restored to narrow gauge, and in the summer of 1947 the army of the Eastern Mongolian Autonomous government was integrated into the Eighth Route army. The autonomy of Hurunbuir passed under Chinese Communist guarantee. However, Chinese Communist participation in the running of the Manchurian railways continued to 1950 only by Soviet grace and favour, as no new agreement with them supplanted the 1945 treaty with the Nationalists.

After the fall of Yenan on 19 March 1947, Manchuria became the most secure Communist base in the civil war. Its trade with the Soviet Union was considerable, and the importance Mao attached to it was indicated by the closeness to himself of the men he appointed to be first secretaries of the Northeastern Party Buro. Lin Biao held the post from mid-1946 to 1949, succeeded by Gao Gang. Soviet writers have claimed that the Manchurian industrial base played the role of a proletarian movement in the Chinese revolution, and was more decisive to the Communist victory than the part of the peasantry. Although the argument is somewhat thin, the importance of Manchuria to the Chinese Communist success should not be under-emphasised. Battered as it was, it contained China's one and only heavy metallurgical industry and a not yet over-populated highly fertile area producing a surplus of farm products.

In general however, the Communists' victory was due to their superior leadership and military strategy, above all to their superior honesty and vision of China's needs. Through land reform and promotion of the people's welfare and women's rights they won the hearts of the masses whom the Nationalists ignored and left to suffer in tremendous oppression and ignorance.

One area where Chinese Communism had little writ until 1949 was Xinjiang. By 1945 Soviet influence was strong over the Muslims of the Ili area. On 31 January 1945, an independent East Turkestan Republic was proclaimed there, which also had virtual control over the Tienshan and Altai mountain regions. But divisions amongst the various Muslim groups prevented them working together effectively against the Nationalist Chinese. Stalin had no wish to get too involved in the province at this stage, or to see any strong Muslim movement creating a focus of interest for its co-religionists of Soviet Central Asia. After the Nationalist government had threatened to raise the Xinjiang question on the international stage (i.e. with Washington and the United Nations), negotiations between the Muslims and Jiang's representatives opened in Urumchi in October 1945, with Soviet consular officials mediating. On 2 January 1946 an eleven-point agreement was signed which abolished the East Turkestan Republic, but gave the minority peoples of Xinjiang a substantial cultural autonomy and an important share in the central provincial government for the first time ever under Chinese rule. From mid-1947 Soviet influence was again reduced to the Ili–Tienshan–Altai area. The Soviet presence there seems to have remained cautious, and the feudal and capitalist classes were not eliminated, but the region had its own army and followed popular welfare policies. Non-Communist indigenes meanwhile continued to work with the Nationalist provincial government in Urumchi. In 1949, with the Nationalist collapse impending, negotiations were started between them and Moscow for a new Xinjiang treaty to replace the 1939 one signed by Sheng Shicai, but Jiang's men would agree to no concessions beyond the continuance of the Sino-Soviet airline. Before anything was finalised the Communists swept to power in China.

Throughout the civil war Soviet press coverage of China and public support for the Communists were limited. Stalin seemed to want to keep China in low key, since the United States was concentrating its anxieties on Europe. In this connection it may be noted that he had drawn remarkably little attention to Korea in the pre-August 1945 discussions with the United States, and it has been surmised that he had hoped to occupy the whole of it had the Americans not at the last moment realised that they must land their forces there. Thus Stalin's China strategy emerges — a careful balance of power between local contenders, lulling of American suspicions, if possible a loss of interest by America, and a free field left for the Soviet Union once it had recovered from the war.

The Chinese Communists were not invited to join the Cominform, the less ambitious successor to the Comintern established in 1947 with the participation only of Soviet bloc, French and Italian Communists. In 1948 Stalin allegedly tried to dissuade Mao from going over to positional warfare and making his all-out bid to overthrow the Nationalists. Moreover, Stalin kept his ambassador with the Nationalist government on its retreat from the mainland right until it reached Canton. But when as late as January 1949 the Nationalists made some appeal to Moscow, this seems to have been spurned by the latter. A similar secret appeal to Washington for assistance by Zhou Enlai on 31 May was no more successful. Mindful of the other card still in Stalin's hand, Mao reiterated his commitment to the Soviet Union when NATO was founded in April 1949, and again on 30 June of that year. He allowed Gao Gang to sign an independent trade treaty with Moscow in July too, on behalf of the Northeastern Party Buro—an act which, coming at a time when the full Chinese Communist victory was already large on the horizon, suggested a Soviet declaration of interest in Manchuria.

Yet in other ways, perhaps mostly by default, Stalin allowed the Communist Chinese to take a rather prominent role in the Asian Communist movement in these years. Mao's foreign policy line of early 1947, voiced by Liu Dingyi, called for an international Communist front headed by the Soviet Union and for wars of liberation in Asia against the capitalist powers. It antedated the similar Soviet Zhdanov line of September 1948 by some 21 months. The Chinese Communists, not the Russians, provided whatever slight foreign backing was received by the Malayan Communist rising. Soviet influence was strong in the Vietnamese and Indonesian parties, but they received no Soviet help and the Indonesian Communists were heavily defeated when they attempted a rising in 1948. The Burmese Communists quickly split into Chinese and Trotskyite groups. As soon as the Chinese Communists took Peking, at the end of September 1949, it became the seat of an important branch of the Soviet-run World Federation of Trade Unions (WFTU), which in some ways assumed a role similar to that of the Cominform in Asia for a few years.

11   1950-1963:

THE ALLIANCE, ITS DEMISE AND BURIAL

On 1 October 1949 Mao proclaimed the Chinese People's Republic in Peking. Already on 30 June he had announced that Communist China would lean to the side of the Soviet Union. Any hope he may have had of US recognition and of playing off the super-powers must have been dashed by the US White Paper of 5 August that year, which castigated both parties to the China struggle in terms so scathing as to make it obvious that the United States had no intention of bothering much more with either, and intended simply to leave mainland China to Stalin, as it in fact did.

Now Mao needed aid, and the Soviet Union with which he already enjoyed good relations was the only possible source. The Russians had got their client China, but not the kind that they would really have liked. It was two and a half months after his triumph that Mao set off for Moscow (and it is observable that he travelled by train, not risking the contrivance of a plane 'accident' by Stalin). The bargaining between the two historic figures took two whole months (although much of it was delegated to secondary men), for Mao alighted in Moscow on 16 December and the first three of the group of treaties and agreements were not signed until 14 February. Remarkably little is still known of what happened in this time.

The 30-year treaty of alliance of 14 February bound the two states to assist one another militarily against Japan or any state aiding Japan in aggression, thus it related only to the East Asian area and did not cover China against American and Nationalist attacks not involving Japan. Soviet credits of US$300 million were extended at 1 per cent for repayment by 1963. In subsidiary agreements the Soviet Union undertook to provide equipment for 50 construction projects over a period of nine years. This aid may be compared with Mao's reputed estimate of US$2-3 billion as

115

necessary to cover China's foreign assistance needs. By 1950 gross industrial production in the Soviet Union already stood at 173 per cent of the 1940 levels, although agricultural output had not regained this level, so lack of generosity to China reflected Soviet political priorities rather than absolute economic necessity.

Further treaties brought further measures of compromise by both sides, as well as gains by the Soviet Union. Mao recognised the independence of Outer Mongolia, but the Soviet government promised to restore the Manchurian railways to China when peace was concluded with Japan or not later than the end of 1952. The same applied to the Lüshun naval base, provided hostilities with Japan had not resumed. The fate of Dalienwan awaited further consultation, though Soviet property there was to be returned to China. In Xinjiang, however, Sino-Soviet joint stock companies were set up, allowing the Russians a share in the rare minerals (including uranium) and oil as well as the civil airline. Another such company was formed in Dalienwan, for shipbuilding.

Foreign policy may have been an important item of discussion between Stalin and Mao, and later in 1950 dramatic developments took place in this field. In a move probably long-planned between Stalin and Kim Ilsung, the North Korean leader, but possibly in the end sprung on Stalin by Kim without warning for internal Korean reasons, the Soviet-trained North Korean army attacked South Korea on 25 June 1950.

Communist China was obliged to intervene militarily in North Korea from 16 October to prevent the arrival of the counter-attacking Americans on the frontiers of Manchuria and the Soviet Maritime Province, and avoid a dangerous confrontation between the armies of the super-powers. Mao pulled Stalin's chestnuts out of the fire on this occasion, and in return the latter did now start partially re-equipping the Chinese forces — military aid having been strikingly omitted from the Sino-Soviet treaties. With Soviet assistance China acquired a force of MIG fighter planes and a small submarine fleet, but it had to pay for the Soviet military hardware. The Korean War greatly worsened relations between China and the United States. Mao lost a son in it, and Washington began to give military support to Taiwan, concluding a military alliance with it in 1955.

Until the death of Stalin there were no noticeable cracks in the Sino-Soviet alliance. The Manchurian railways were returned on time, and the Soviet Union provided indispensable military cover and technological assistance of many kinds to the new Communist state. Soviet aid in the outcome proved rather more all-embracing and generous than the stingy first treaties had suggested. China's trade rapidly became heavily orientated towards the Soviet Union and numbers of Chinese went there for university study or technical training. In 1953 Mao himself called for a tidal wave of learning from the Soviet Union, which certainly happened. In these early years the Soviet model was followed by China in all professional matters, except to some extent military, and most thoroughly in the northeast and Xinjiang where Soviet influence was greatest. The Muslim minorities in the latter province were even allowed to continue using a Cyrillic alphabet. By September 1953 the Russians were helping to build and equip a total of 141 enterprises in China.

Yet in many ways Chinese Communism from the Jiangxi-Soviet period until recently differed distinctly from Russian, and not only in the way in which it came to power. In the private personal sphere the standards successfully imposed on the nation at this time—though some of the leaders did not entirely practice what they preached—were highly puritanical, unlike the unofficial libertarianism which ever since 1917 had been overtaking the Russians as it had other industrial nations. Since the whole technique of coming to power in China had been based on the peasants, until 1958 at least the emphasis on peasant welfare was higher in China than in Russia, where the peasants had not been directly responsible for the Bolshevik revolution and under Stalin were grossly exploited in the interests of industrial investment. The dire mistakes of collectivisation in Russia were avoided in China in the early and mid-1950s. Above all, Mao, who unlike Lenin before the October revolution had accumulated long experience of government during the Yenan and civil war years, addressed himself far more seriously to the problems of re-educating the people to a Communist system. Instead of relying mainly on the secret police to enforce outward conformity, as even Lenin to some degree and Stalin notoriously had done, the Chinese Communists tried to refashion their people's thinking by an endless series of persuasion campaigns, backed by force, but not with the arbitrary savagery of Stalin's Russia. The importance attached to moral persuasion was quite in the Confucian tradition of government, and Mao's own political thinking differed sharply from Lenin's and Stalin's in this respect. Lenin had expected that the basic problems of politics and society would be soon resolved by socialist reforms and economic progress (and began to realise his mistake too late), whereas Stalin (no great political thinker) had largely closed his eyes to the fact that they had not — or perhaps, with his low social and educational background, was relatively little aroused by such problems. Mao, on the other hand, believed that contradictions would continue in socialist society for a long time, and must be periodically eradicated by new revolutionary shake-ups. His theory of contradictions underlay the whole of his complexly interwoven thought and political practice. Another difference lay in the policy towards the middle classes. In Soviet Russia many of these had been blithely driven away in the wave of internationalist proletarian euphoria of 1917–19, but in China only the landlord class was destroyed and its descendants persecuted. The bourgeoisie were courted for the contribution they could make to their country's development. Even the leaders of other Chinese left-wing parties were tamed for use by the regime, instead of being eliminated as in Russia. And at bottom the Chinese revolution was from the start far more nationalist than the Russian had been in its early, Leninist phase, for Russia had never been the victim of imperialism in the way China had been.

On 5 March 1953 Stalin died: a russified Georgian revolutionary statesman also in the tradition of the most appalling of Asian tyrants, or a ferocious sixteenth-century Russian tsar, Ivan the Terrible. He left the Soviet Union second only to the United States in industrial power, yet politically demoralised and beleaguered diplomatically within the Soviet bloc, with scant friends outside it. His death brought considerable changes to Soviet politics. After a short, fairly discreet power struggle Khrushchev emerged as his successor, by contrast to Stalin an ordinary Russian writ just a little large, who never inspired the same awe in anyone and certainly not in Mao Zedong. The Soviet secret police were demoted from their overweening position and their chief, Berea, was shot. The Soviet Communist Party regained its leading role and relations with the West began to relax.

By common consent of the ruling group, the Soviet government sought to remake its international image: the leaders travelled freely abroad like any Western statesmen, abandoning Stalin's heavily guarded existence. The new and growing economic might of the Union was used more and more to win influence in the West and the Third World, a large navy and merchant marine were developed and a more pacific foreign policy laid down.

More aid was given to China in fresh agreements in 1953, and still more in October 1954 when Khrushchev came personally to Peking. He then agreed to sell China the Soviet shares in the joint stock companies, and some observers consider he enlisted Mao's support in his struggle for power in Moscow. The Manchurian ports were returned to China on 25 May 1955, the period of their retention by the Russians having been prolonged with Chinese consent.

But not long after Stalin's death some divergence in Soviet and Chinese policies became apparent, especially in foreign affairs. In April 1954 the Chinese Foreign Minister Zhou Enlai proclaimed the Five Principles of Peaceful Co-existence with the Indian Premier Nehru, marking a new drive by China to win friends in Asia, which was soon to bring it into rivalry with the Soviet Union. At the Geneva Conference on Indo-China between April and July 1954, China gave much more backing to the Vietmin than Moscow did. Molotov and Eden brought about a settlement by acting as brokers reconciling the views of Washington and Peking. No Soviet support at all was forthcoming for Peking's attempt to invade Taiwan in September, which got no further than the bombardment of Quemoy. The Bandung Afro-Asian Conference of April 1955 saw the Soviet Union excluded and China taking a prominent part. Independent and very low-key talks were started in Geneva between US and Chinese representatives in 1955, lasting until 1958. China's first Five Year Plan, begun in 1954, devoted an even higher percentage of investment to industry than had the first Soviet one of 1929, another pointer to things to come. Sometime that year the disgrace of Gao Gang, who had been made head of the State Planning Commission in 1953 and was associated with strong advocacy of Soviet organisational models, marked the start of a turning-away from these. Gao later killed himself. These circumstances were at one time believed to indicate a close Soviet link on his part, one writer postulating a tie-up between him and Berea, but the consensus seems now to discount this.

The real trouble began with the Soviet Twentieth Party Congress in April 1956. This was the scene of Khrushchev's famous denunciation of Stalin for his treatment of the party and of agriculture—not for his reign of terror against the Soviet people. Khrushchev also enunciated the new principles of foreign policy, indicating that the Soviet Union would no longer try to enforce its tactics on other Communist parties, and that in contrast to Lenin's views transition to socialism was possible without revolution, and wars with the capitalist world no longer inevitable as Lenin had judged them to be. This set the stage for much more liberal measures at home, for coming to terms with the United States and for a Soviet drive for influence with the bourgeois nationalist governments of the Third World. Henceforth for many years Moscow was to make active use of Communist parties only when it found governments intractable, or very ripe for toppling. None of this was acceptable to Mao, especially as he had not been consulted beforehand. The ideological dispute between him and the Russians now began to take shape, centring mainly on Mao's theory of contradictions, his claim to be the senior thinker of the Communist bloc, and his adherence to the old Leninist line on revolution and the certainty of war between socialist and capitalist states. Moreover the relevance of Soviet models, in literature at least, had already been found questionable for Chinese circumstances by this date and had been abandoned. From about this time, major Soviet Communist Party directives were also no longer made required study for the higher levels of the Chinese Party.

Yet for the present the Chinese still needed the Soviet Union and Khrushchev still needed the Chinese. Within the next three years he wound up most of Stalin's concentration camps, amnestied many prisoners and embarked on a programme of major improvement in the state of the collective farmers. A relaxation towards writers and the Eastern European countries had already begun earlier. This led to a violent anti-Soviet uprising in Hungary in October 1956, and a crisis in Poland where an uprising was probably narrowly averted when Moscow allowed the national Communist Gomulka to become leader in place of the Stalinist Ochab. China's political weight was valuable as a back-up to Moscow in this situation, and was forthcoming on its own terms. Peking apparently approved the bloody crushing of the Hungarian rising by the Soviet army, but counselled moderation towards the Poles, who had not shown signs of rebellion against their Communist Party as such, but only against its Stalinist leadership. In short, China took a stance supportive of the Polish party. In January 1957 Zhou Enlai visited Budapest, Warsaw and Moscow, and issued a joint communique with the Soviet government ostensibly backing it to the hilt. Yet diplomatically useful as this was, Moscow can hardly have hoped that it was a precedent for further Chinese participation in Eastern European affairs.

The Soviet Union had already exploded its first hydrogen bomb in 1953 and launched its first ICBM in 1955. Now in 1957 it became the first country to put an earth satellite into orbit. The vast expansion of Soviet military power which these things heralded prompted the Chinese leaders to urge a more aggressive foreign policy on Moscow — including, perhaps, a joint bid to take Taiwan. They began, it seems, to canvass sections of the Soviet industrial and military establishment in support of their views, to the great annoyance of the Kremlin. And the Chinese advice fell on deaf ears, for the Russians were now more mindful of the destructive possibilities of their new weapons and in any case knew that they were still well behind the Americans in armaments. Khrushchev, however, overcame his opponents in the Soviet leadership — the so-called 'anti-Party group' — in 1957, according to some writers with some help from Mao, to whom perhaps by way of repayment he 'promised' a sample nuclear bomb, possibly after Mao had attended the Bolshevik revolution celebrations in Moscow that year.

All direct Soviet credits to China had been spent by the end of 1957 and no new direct ones were forthcoming, but a new increased trade agreement was concluded in April 1958. It is said that the Russians were pressing China to integrate its economy fully with that of the Soviet bloc by joining CEMA (Council for Economic Mutual Assistance of Soviet-bloc countries) and signing a long-term trade agreement. In July of this year Khrushchev and his defence minister went to Peking with further demands for a joint control over Chinese atomic research and the Chinese navy, and over a new military radar system to be created in China with Soviet aid. These demands were angrily rejected, but to placate the Chinese Khrushchev agreed to supply substantially more industrial equipment, vehicles and petroleum and to equip 47 new enterprises. On 15 October a technological agreement was signed under which China acquired some nuclear know-how.

Khrushchev was apparently staking much on securing a nuclear deal with the United States and at the same time preventing both China and West Germany from obtaining nuclear weapons. Mao for his part had new plans to free his country from Soviet tutelage and convert it at high speed into a great industrial power. In August 1958 without prior word to Moscow the Commune movement and the Great Leap Forward were launched in China together with the Mao cult. This had been preceded by the so-called Hundred Flowers Movement, a short-lived relaxation of press censorship in China (March–June 1957) which led to an outburst of complaints against the regime, coupled with some attacks on Soviet policies in the Peking press, although no criticism of anything Soviet was allowed in the provincial papers.

In essence, the Great Leap was an attempt to out-Stalin Stalin's economic policies by eliminating the private element from the people's lives entirely, abolishing private plots, introducing communal feeding, and turning the whole adult population to work in agriculture, industry, or innumerable small back-yard factories where iron and steel as well as many other industrial goods were to be produced. To generate the necessary enthusiasm, Mao was elevated virtually to a god in a manner exceeding even the adulation which had been demanded for Stalin in the Soviet Union. The whole was presented to the world as a new, better and faster way to Communism.

Moscow viewed this with barely concealed dismay. If it succeeded, China might rapidly eclipse the Soviet Union, and if it failed, as was more likely, the Soviet Union might have to relieve the ensuing disaster. The Great Leap was marked by a general turning-away from the Soviet Union in China. Soviet models in military training, never exclusively used, were totally abandoned, and many Soviet journals were no longer subscribed to. Joint development projects on the Amur were suspended, although possibly at Soviet initiative. Soviet influence over the Muslim minority intelligentsia in the Ili area of Xinjiang began to be progressively rooted out. In September 1958 China carried out the second bombardment of Quemoy, and once again no Soviet support was forthcoming, nor was the invasion attempted.

By the end of 1958 the foreign and domestic policies of China and the Soviet Union had effectively diverged. Khrushchev was bent on an understanding with Washington, but the Chinese had broken off their Geneva talks with the Americans and were back in an attitude of hostility towards them. The Soviet Union was drawing closer to India at this time when tension was rising between that country and China over border problems. Neither Moscow nor Peking however wanted to make a complete break. China still needed Soviet aid, and Khrushchev for his part still hoped to control China enough to prevent it getting the nuclear bomb. In January 1959 he is said to have proposed a Pacific atom free zone, but Peking would agree only if the Soviet Union itself participated. Despite a new technical and economic aid agreement in February for 5 billion roubles worth of Soviet goods and services to build 78 more large plants by 1967 — the most extensive so far — Khrushchev cancelled his offer of a sample nuclear bomb to Peking on 20 June.

A criticism of the Great Leap made to Mao on 14 July by Chinese Defence Minister Peng Dehuai was thought at one time to have had direct links to Khruschev, who also attacked the Leap in a speech in Poland on 21 July. Yet although Peng was soon dismissed and many aspects of the case remain unexplained, it now seems more likely that it was devoid of any deep significance in the Sino-Soviet context.

Rivalry towards the Third World, particularly in Indonesia, sharpened meanwhile, and when the Sino-Indian war broke out in September 1959 the Soviet Union disavowed the Chinese position. On 16 September Khrushchev had an historic Camp David meeting with President Eisenhower, thus presenting to the Chinese the classic example of collusion with their worst enemy, the United States. But after barely touching down in Moscow, Khrushchev dashed to Peking in October on his third and last visit, to try to smooth things over. It proved useless, for the Chinese leaders became more and more hostile in their attitude towards Moscow, although the outside world as yet knew little of this. A long militant statement of Mao's views in the dispute published in Peking on the nineteth anniversary of Lenin's birth on 22 April 1960 did not directly attack the Soviet Union. Both sides had been veiling the quarrel from capitalist eyes — though most likely not from those of politically experienced Communists — by the device of using Yugoslavia and Albania as stalking horses for oblique onslaughts on each other. The Chinese had begun to vilify Yugoslavia in this way as early as May 1958, and the Russians followed suit with Albania, with which their relations had deteriorated since 1956.

In New Delhi in February 1960 Khrushchev in person signed a

treaty with India, to which country Moscow had given nearly US$800 million credits by the end of the year, and on 31 May the Chinese countered by concluding a friendship treaty with the Soviet satellite of Outer Mongolia, with a loan of $200 million. Later in the year Albania put itself under Chinese protection, its 'little Stalin' Enver Hoxha having been alarmed by an unsuccessful Soviet plot to overthrow him and by the Soviet *rapproachement* with his enemy Yugoslavia. Another historic milestone of sinister purport to Moscow had been reached, and China had its first European satellite.

Despite the collapse of the Soviet-American Geneva summit meeting that month because of the shooting down of the US U-2 spy-plane over the Soviet Union, Khrushchev summarily withdrew all the Soviet scientists and specialists from China in the same month. By the end of August some 1390 of them had gone home, taking with them many valuable blueprints, thus striking a great blow at China's industrial development. From this point the Sino-Soviet alliance factually ceased to exist, although attempts to revive it were not to be finally abandoned until the summer of 1963.

Khrushchev's withdrawal of the Soviet advisers came at a moment when the Chinese economy was already shaken by the failure of the Great Leap Forward. He perhaps intended to give the *coup de grace* to the current Peking leadership and produce one more amenable to Moscow. For the Great Leap had dislocated China's planning and statistical system, disrupted food growing, disgruntled the population and completely failed to produce the expected tide of industrial production of useful quality. Natural disasters in 1959–60 compounded the trouble. Mao fell under something of a cloud, and the more pragmatic if less charismatic Liu Shaochi began to assume more prominence as chairman of the Chinese People's Republic from 1959, although Mao remained party chairman and carried greater authority in foreign policy and ideology in the last resort. They continued in this way as almost twin stars in the Chinese political firmament until the Cultural Revolution.

In retrospect, the ten-year alliance with the Russians had given China the following: some 10 800 carefully selected Soviet experts had served there, generally leaving behind them a good memory of their efforts as individuals, as far as can be ascertained; 6000–7000 Chinese had received higher education in the Soviet

Union and more than 38 000 had received specialist training there (Chinese students in the Soviet Union in 1960 were allowed to finish their courses); China had learnt to build various kinds of armaments, including fighter planes and submarines of Soviet design and had gained some basic expertise in the use of nuclear energy; and to the end of 1960 Moscow had given China loans of US$450 million and total credits and aid to the value of US$2250 million. But in the same period total Soviet aid to other Third World countries had amounted to considerably more than this, and China itself had proffered about half the amount it received from Moscow to other countries, including North Korea. Of 336 major industrial enterprises started with Soviet aid in China, only 198 were completed. Moreover, there were repeated Chinese complaints later that the Soviet Union did not often send its most advanced types of equipment and machinery to China, nor, when they were sent, did these often compare well with the best the world had to offer in this period. The military hardware was particularly criticised by the Chinese. The Russians on the other hand felt that they had given China as much as they safely could, whilst it is hard to see that they had gained much from the alliance except for the Korean War bonus and the exclusion of American influence. China had declined to accept the role of satellite integrated into the Soviet bloc. Thus the application of Soviet aid had left both sides with grievances, apart from their national and ideological differences.

In 1960 over half China's trade was with the Soviet Union and its debts to Russia amounted to 560 million roubles, of which 62 per cent was for military supplies. This had crushing implications for a desperately poor country in the throes of food shortage and manifold difficulties. Yet the Peking government decided to pay off the debts to Moscow, and the withdrawal of the Soviet specialists brought only a slight measure of capitulation from China. Liu Shaochi apparently advocated the maintenance of the Soviet tie, despite Mao's opposition. The Chinese politburo laid the groundwork for deradicalisation in domestic policy in November 1960, but this was not done in response to any direct Soviet pressure. Subsequently the communes were wound up in the cities and in the countryside a temporary return to a market economy took place in conditions of great stress and hunger. Some of the reforms of the Great Leap were retained and others abandoned in a reversion to more Soviet-type practices. Peasants' private plots were allowed again.

Liu Shaochi led the Chinese delegation to the Congress of 81 Communist Parties in Moscow in November–December, staged by the Russians in an effort to win approval for their new foreign policy lines. The Soviet spokesmen formulated the idea of national democracy as a halfway stage between bourgeois governments and socialism in the Third World, the implication being that such regimes, should they emerge, would be Soviet satellites. Despite a violent personal quarrel between Khrushchev and Deng Xiaoping (then secretary general of the Chinese Communist Party, a less important post than that of the same name in the Soviet Union), the Congress approved a closing declaration embodying Moscow's views.

Relations thereafter somewhat improved. There was a lull in the attacks on Yugoslavia and Albania. In February 1961 a Soviet economic mission arrived in Peking and the anniversary of the alliance was celebrated in both capitals. There was even talk of a return of the Soviet advisers. Although China could not meet the terms of the 1958 and 1959 trade treaties, a new trade agreement in April was fairly lenient to it, for Moscow postponed repayment of US$320 million of China's debts for five years, and half a million tons of sugar was supplied on interest-free credit. Completion by the Russians of the railway from Aktogai in Soviet Kazakhstan to the Chinese frontier at the Jungarian pass in Xinjiang took place later that year, though the linking line on the Chinese side was never made. China played a rather conciliatory part in the renewed Geneva conference on Laos, which met intermittently between May 1961 and July 1962. Summoned by the United States because its Laotian protégé, the rightist General Phoumi, was endangered by the China and Vietmin-backed Pathet Lao movement, the conference resulted in a brief period of neutrality in Laos, which corresponded more or less to Soviet wishes and not Chinese.

In the early 1960s the Soviet Union itself was experiencing economic problems, although of a much less serious kind than China's. Industrial growth rates had dropped to the lowest figure since 1933, with GNP growth at only 4.2 per cent in 1963 and 1964. Khrushchev had launched the country into a series of ill-planned reforms, abolishing the economic ministries and establishing inadequately co-ordinated regional economic councils. In 1963 he even proposed splitting the Party into industrial and agricultural halves. His relaxation of labour laws and of terror probably helped to reduce work discipline too. In addition to this Khrushchev's main attention was still fixed on America and the nuclear proliferation problem. He continued to pursue this line with Peking, and with President Kennedy at the Vienna summit meeting of June 1961. After this his hardening attitude to the United States, including a flamboyant series of nuclear tests in the atmosphere and the building of the Berlin wall, has been interpreted by some as a bid to please China and regain some control over its foreign policy, but was probably more directed to the United States and the flight of population from East Germany.

In any case according to Soviet sources Liu Shaochi turned against the Soviet tie sometime in 1961 and the Twenty-second Congress of the Soviet Communist Party in October of that year saw a definite worsening of relations. Zhou Enlai, the Chinese representative, denounced the United States, Khrushchev publicly repeated his attacks on Stalin, and Zhou left early after placing a wreath on Stalin's grave. The Congress approved Khrushchev's new party programme, which declared that class struggle had ended in the Soviet Union where the party was now recognised as the vanguard of the whole nation and no longer purely proletarian. The Soviet state was no longer a dictatorship of the proletariat but a state of all the working people. In face of this, Mao began to develop the doctrine that the abandonment of the dictatorship of the proletariat left the road open in Russia for the formation of new exploiting classes and the restoration of a bureaucratic form of capitalism. From this point both sides began to use the ideological dispute as a weapon to destroy each other's domestic legitimacy as well as international status.

In 1962 there was a serious crisis in Xinjiang, where measures taken by the Chinese against the Muslims led to several tens of thousands of Kazakhs and Uigurs fleeing to the Soviet Union with the active encouragement of Soviet Intelligence and the Soviet consuls, who freely issued Soviet passports and even had them sold on the black market. In retaliation, Peking closed all the remaining Soviet consulates in China in mid-September, and esoteric media attacks on the Soviet Union by China and direct ones by Albania were resumed.

In June Jiang Kaishek appeared poised to launch an attack on the mainland, but this move, whilst it may have been encouraged by sections of the US leadership, was quashed by President Kennedy. Moscow gave only verbal support to China after the danger was passed. But when China again became involved in war with India over border infringements in October (by pure coincidence at the same time as the Cuban missile crisis), Moscow gave slightly more approval than in 1959. China's proposals for a cease-fire on 24 October were endorsed by Moscow, even though the conditions were rather humiliating for India. When the Chinese asked for unequivocal backing from Moscow and the Indian Communist Party on 27 October, this was initially forthcoming from the former, and Peking for its part initially backed the Soviet position in the Cuban missile crisis.

Cuba had passed through a revolution led by Fidel Castro, becoming an ally of the Soviet Union in 1959, and the missile crisis appears to have been the crux of Khrushchev's wild scheme for a simultaneous solution to the problem of America and nuclear proliferation. By stationing the nuclear missiles on Cuba, within easy reach of the United States, he hoped to force Kennedy to do a deal on nuclear arms, to agree to deny them to Germany and perhaps to abandon his protection of Taiwan, in return for removal of the missiles and the renunciation of nuclear arms by China. As is well known, the plan miscarried and the missiles were removed in return only for an undertaking by Kennedy not to attack Cuba. Yet thus the Soviet Union acquired a secure if expensive base in the Western hemisphere, whilst the Chinese gained nothing except an endorsement of their freedom to 'go nuclear' on their own.

The Chinese made propaganda out of the Soviet discomfiture, sharing Castro's objections to the removal of the missiles. Moscow reverted to a pro-Indian stance in the Sino-Indian war, which continued to a virtual Chinese victory and withdrawal to the original frontier on 21 November. Before the end of the year the Sino-Soviet dispute had begun to escalate once more. Nevertheless Sino-Mongolian relations, which had begun to improve in 1961, did not yet deteriorate again. It was noteworthy that China concluded a thorough frontier delimitation treaty with the Mongolian People's Republic in December 1962 as well as a similar treaty with Pakistan. The treaty with Mongolia would probably not have been concluded without Soviet approval, and was accompanied in the same period by the signing of various agreements providing for economic aid from China, particularly for the provision of Chinese labour for construction projects in Mongolia. But to counter the possible Chinese pull, Moscow allowed the MPR to become a full member of CEMA in 1962.

In January 1963 the Chinese for the first time attacked Khrushchev openly by name. Open polemics were taking place on both sides by February, and on 8 March the Peking press raised the question of the unequal treaties imposed on China by Russia in the past. After this incidents began to multiply on the Sino-Soviet frontiers, one of the few parts of the frontiers of either state which had never been given a proper modern demarcation.

China was emerging as the patron of revolution and attacking the Soviet Union as a revisionist back-slider from the cause of the world's oppressed masses. In March 1963 Peking launched the Three Spheres of the World theory, intimating that it was now challenging the Russians in the Third World with a vengeance. Most Asian Communist parties supported China at this point, and its influence was rising in North Vietnam and Indonesia. Liu Shaochi visited both in the spring of 1963, backing Sukarno's Konfrontasi campaign against the joining of the former British North Borneo colonies to independent Malaya to form Malaysia. Liu also encouraged the guerrilla war developing against South Vietnam. Chinese and Albanian demonstrations at the World Women's Congress in Moscow on 29 June led to the expulsion of some but not all Chinese diplomats and students from the Soviet Union.

Abortive Sino-Soviet talks held in Moscow from 5 to 20 July were perhaps a blame-fixing manoeuvre by each side. The corpse of the alliance, after lying about since 1960, was by this means at last given an unofficial funeral. No more attempts were made to revive it and there followed a flood of open recriminations and revelations from both countries, continuing for years. When the United States, Britain and the Soviet Union signed the Partial Test Ban Treaty on 25 July 1963, and the hot line between the White House and the Kremlin was thereafter inaugurated, the two super-powers stood somewhat closer to one another than either did to China. Yet the need to compete with China for the allegiance of the Communist parties made it impossible for Moscow to reach the full accord with Washington which its interests at that time might have suggested.

12   1963-1969:

CHINESE REVOLUTIONARY
FERVOUR AND SOVIET
CONTAINMENT

China had flung down the gauntlet to the Soviet Union and was set to challenge it on a world-wide stage. At the close of the year Zhou Enlai with 50 officials visited ten African and three Asian countries and Albania. Chinese influence was already marked in Congo Brazzaville (the former French Congo) by 1963 and was actively sought in other places on the perimeter of the former Belgian Congo as well as in East Africa. Zhou returned home with an optimistic report on revolutionary prospects in Africa. But at the World Peace Congress in Warsaw in December 1963, China's militant anti-Western line and bid to wrest the leadership of the Third World delegations from the Soviet Union were defeated. At no time, moreover, did China's support for anti-Soviet and anti-Western movements exceed the bounds of trade, aid and verbal support.

Nearer home 1963 was still a difficult year for the Chinese. The grain harvest was very disappointing, and Peking was obliged as for the past two years to buy 3 million tons of grain abroad. The Soviet Union on the other hand, with a crop failure too, was able with its greater resources to buy as much as 12 million tons of grain from overseas and began to recover from the temporary setbacks of the Cuban crisis and the break with China. A slight upward movement in the GNP growth had taken place (to 5 per cent) and its standard of living was beginning to improve. In the Middle East particularly and in the Third World generally Soviet stature was slowly increasing. By now the U.S.S.R. was becoming a predominantly urban and industrial country: in the early 1960s the urban population for the first time exceeded the rural, and thenceforth steadily increased in proportion to it.

The beginning of 1964, however, saw a small success for China: France recognised the People's Republic, abandoning its support for Taiwan. Both de Gaulle, then French president, and Peking had reason to dislike the Soviet-American entente, but de Gaulle's recognition was aimed primarily to lead, as it did, to closer ties between the Soviet Union and France.

With the spring of 1964 the ideological dispute was full-blown, two complete alternative interpretations of Marxism-Leninism being offered to the world. The Soviet version, contained in the Open Letter to all Communist parties on 12 February, was based on Khrushchev's 1961 party programme; the Chinese version was laid out in a series of commentaries on this, especially the ninth commentary of 14 July, entitled 'On Khrushchev's phoney Communism'. These commentaries embodied the later ideas of Mao, calling for ever new revolutions in China to prevent it sinking into what he perceived as the Soviet pattern of bureaucratic inequality, consumerism and compromise with the capitalists.

Under the impact of this, the world Communist movemnet began to break up. By the end of the 1960s pro-Chinese parties had split off from the Communist parties in many countries, including Australia, Belgium, Brazil, Ceylon, Columbia, India, Japan, Lebanon, Nepal and Paraguay. The Indonesian party (PKI) swung more to Peking in the early 1960s, but was crushed, as we shall see, in 1965. All the pro-Chinese new parties were to remain rather small and weak compared to the parent bodies and the main long-term effect was to make all the strong parties more independent of both China and the Soviet Union. An exception to this may, however, be seen in the Indian party, which seems to have remained loyal to Moscow.

For the rest of 1964 the Chinese stepped up their challenge, supplying arms to the Congo rebels in competition with the Russians and seeking to improve their governmental relations with West Germany, India and Japan. The Soviet Party Central Committee debated the China problem on 14 and 15 February, from which a consensus apparently emerged that Mao must if possible be overthrown. In the light of hindsight, it may be hypothesised that the border talks that started between the two countries on 25 February were intended by Moscow to offer a programme of reasonable concessions and constructive suggestions for better relations, which could be used by the opponents of Mao as an argument for a reversal of policy towards the Soviet Union.

These talks soon failed, however, and on 10 July Mao threw the border issue in the face of the world, in a way no Soviet government could forgive, by telling Japanese journalists in Peking that the Soviet Union was an imperialist state, which had wrongfully taken the Kuriles from Japan and territory from Finland, East Germany, Poland and Rumania, as well as China.

Some historians have attributed the fall from power of Khrushchev on 14 October 1964 to the disapproval of senior colleagues at his supposed contemplated military action against China. Others have credited his weak handling of the world parties against China with being the final straw, especially in the case of Suslov, the man mainly responsible for replacing him with Brezhnev. The published evidence is so far inconclusive, and in any case the Soviet leadership's annoyance with Khrushchev's chaotic internal policies is a sufficient explanation for his downfall.

Khrushchev was succeeded by a triumvirate of serious, able men, of whom Brezhnev, the party general secretary, was the leader. A master machine politican without Khrushchev's colourful peasant originality and imagination, he was better educated, more dignified, astute and cautious, with a special interest in foreign policy. Ideological and cultural matters he left mainly to the elder statesman Suslov, who had declined his colleagues' offer of the top position in favour of a role behind Brezhnev's chair. Supervision of the economy became basically the task of Prime Minister Kosygin, since the titular head of state, Podgorny, was of less weight than the others. This group was well assisted by the foreign minister since the end of 1956, Gromyko (still in the post in 1982).

Under Brezhnev, the Soviet ruling circles were to present a picture of unity and tight secrecy over all policy debates in contrast to the ever-continuing arguments and manoeuvres for power' in China, where the much greater magnitude of the problems faced gave rise to correspondingly greater differences of opinion on policy. Soviet foreign policy continued to unfold on the lines laid down at the Twentieth Party Congress, re-stated by Brezhnev himself after the Twenty-third Party Congress in March 1966. Brezhnev's China policy to 1982 appeared to consist in seeking measures to contain it without pushing it to desperation, and to re-establish working relations if possible under a more pliant Chinese leadership.

Perhaps not by accident, the Chinese chose to conduct their

first nuclear test at about the time Khrushchev fell, but they welcomed the new men at the helm in the Kremlin with prompt greetings. A short-lived detente immediately took place in Sino-Soviet relations. Zhou Enlai was sent to represent Peking at the November revolution celebrations, at which Brezhnev outlined his policy, offering to resume technological and even military aid to China in return for China's co-operation to some extent in foreign affairs. He also forecast a more vigorous Soviet policy in Asia. No response came from the Chinese leaders, who perhaps felt on the verge of a great breakthrough in their own foreign policy schemes now that their country had recovered somewhat from its economic and climatic disasters. Chinese influence with the governments of Indonesia and Pakistan was in fact growing, leading to the former quitting the United Nations in January 1965, when Peking called for a new revolutionary UN to be set up. This never materialised, but the wraith of a Peking–Jakarta–Karachi axis seemed visible, sufficient to alarm both Washington and Moscow. China also recognised the Palestinian fedayeen in a bid to promote Chinese influence in the Middle East, at a time when the Soviet Union had not recognised them and was to avoid doing so until 1974.

Yet the year was to go against China in world politics. Chinese influence suffered a debacle in several African countries, although Tanzania accepted its offer to build a railway linking Tanzania's Indian Ocean port with Zambian iron mines, thus freeing Zambia from dependence on railways leading to South African ports for its iron exports. The Afro-Asian Algiers Conference set for June, on which Peking had placed great hopes as a forum, never met owing to the overthrow of Boumedienne by Ben Bella, and the Third World as a whole turned against the Chinese as a result of their demands that it should make enemies of both America and the Soviet Union. A small Communist conference of 26 parties summoned in Moscow in March was boycotted by China and the few important parties which still adhered to her — the North Korean, Japanese, Indonesian and North Vietnamese — and also by three neutralist parties including the Rumanian. The loss of even North Vietnam to Chinese influence can also possibly be traced back to this time, for the commencement of US air raids on North Vietnam on 7 February compelled the Soviet Union to begin providing it with military aid. Moscow could not face the loss of prestige which it would have suffered from the defeat of Vietnam by the United States or Vietnam's rescue by China, nor could the Russians have tolerated the boost to Chinese power which the latter outcome might have brought. But Peking was not prepared to co-operate in the transport of Soviet aid to Vietnam across Chinese territory without a settlement of its differences with Moscow on its own terms, so fresh controversies arose.

Then in August and September the Peking–Jakarta–Karachi axis suffered a still-birth. During the Indo-Pakistan war over Kashmir in these months Peking gave the Pakistanis much verbal incitement, but they fought half-heartedly and the war ended in stalemate. Finally, on 30 September the Indonesian generals moved against the pro-Chinese Sukarno and the PKI, which led to an enormous massacre of Indonesian Communists by their Muslim fellow-countrymen, in East Java particularly. At least 100 000 — some say 300 000 — perished, and the PKI has not recovered to this day. The Indonesian army took over the country, inaugurating a close understanding with the United States.

China's premature bid to challenge the Soviet Union for leadership in the Communist movement and to defy both super-powers in the Third World generally had failed by the end of 1965, whilst the Russians were getting into an easier stride under their new rulers. These had wound up Khrushchev's unpopular party reform and economic decentralisation, and embarked on a new programme of limited moves towards a market economy, with devolution of control over industrial transactions, greater investment in research and technology, and increased armament spending. The strategy of the new leaders in domestic affairs seemed to lie in producing not only more guns but also more butter, both increasing armaments and raising the standard of living, which they were able to accomplish through the continued steady if unspectacular rise in the GNP during the 1960s and the detente with America. The latter permitted them virtually to institutionalise their annual purchases of vast quantities of grain from Canada as well as the United States, to the point where North American farmers came partially to depend on the Russian market. The inefficiency and climatic handicaps of Soviet agriculture were thus bypassed, and a new leverage on the United States developed, albeit one which could work both ways to some extent.

Another important development of 1965 in the Soviet Union was the start of a great build-up of armed forces on the borders with China, which had been relatively lightly defended up to this time. By 1968 there were to be fifteen Soviet divisions there.

Already the revolutionary impulses of Mao and those of his fellow countrymen who followed his domestic line had begun to turn inward against other Chinese. Lin Biao's *Peking Review* article 'Long live the victory of People's War' on 3 September 1965 not only ushered in the Great Cultural Revolution in China but a period of more passive Chinese foreign policy, the theory of which was that China should wait as an isolated revolutionary fortress for the 'World Countryside' (the Third World) to surround and destroy the 'World Town' of the rich nations. (This idea was not entirely new, having some resemblance to Li Dazhao's proletarian nations theory of 1920, and the similar views of the Soviet Tatar national Communist Sultan Galiev in 1918.)

Mao's Cultural Revolution was aimed in stages at 'feudal survivals', the entrenched Chinese party and bureaucracy, the educational system, and the position of his rival Liu Shaochi with his supporters, the mayor of Peking Peng Zhen and the Communist Party secretary Deng Xiaoping. To carry it through, Mao enlisted above all the surplus energies of China's youth. Enrolled as Red Guards, they terrorised the universities and schools and the supporters of Liu, and destroyed many priceless treasures of art and architecture in the name of destroying feudalism. China fell into chaos, and by January 1967 something like a real worker revolution was taking place in Shanghai, with proletarian factions seizing control of factories. Intermittently and in the end, in 1968, decisively, Mao himself had to call in the army to restore order.

The China of the Cultural Revolution presented to foreign observers the same sort of picture of revolutionary insanity that was conveyed to the outside world by the Paris of 1793–94 or the Russia of the 1930s. In all three cases, a revolution had reached its most feverish pitch of endeavour, and the relative isolation of its participants from the rest of the world had induced a qualitative difference in their sense of values compared to those of the calmer lands abroad. It is no coincidence that all three periods were followed by far-reaching relaxations of tension (though in the Soviet case this did not come until Stalin's death).

Meanwhile the Soviet government continued to pursue goals of pure national interest abroad. January 1966 had seen Soviet prestige in South Asia much enhanced by Kosygin's successful mediation of the Indo-Pakistan peace conference held in Tashkent. Yet neither the debates at the Tri-Continental Conference in Havana in January nor those involving the foreign Communist representatives at the Twenty-third Soviet Party Congress in March were exactly a triumph for Moscow. Its prestige in the world Communist movement was tarnished, and henceforth its successes were to be those of power rather than of ideology.

Sino-Soviet inter-party relations were finally severed after Peking's rejection on 22 March of an invitation to the Twenty-third Party Congress in Moscow. A last attempt by Rumania to reconcile China and the Soviet Union in June proved fruitless. Border incidents proliferated, Red Guards rioted outside the Soviet embassy in Peking on 29 August 1966, foreign students were expelled from China in September and most of the remaining Chinese students from the Soviet Union in October — but even then not all. A plenary meeting of the Central Committee of the Soviet Communist Party in midsummer condemned Mao and all his works, and the Soviet government formed a Xinjiang Muslim army from the reputed 200 000 refugees who fled from Chinese territory in 1962. Yet the minimum inter-state relations between the two countries continued. The commission on navigation on the Manchurian border rivers continued to function. A civil aviation agreement was signed on 4 April, and a technical and scientific co-operation agreement on 6 November. The shipments of Soviet aid to North Vietnam through China involved some co-operation. Such things might be compared to the ongoing dealings over the Russian Orthodox mission in the dark days of eighteenth-century tension between the Qing and tsarist empires.

The year 1967 saw the climax of the Cultural Revolution, as far as its external impact was concerned. In this phase ultra-left elements unleashed against foreigners on China's soil and foreign governments to which China's embassies were accredited a kind of substitute for the full-scale revolutionary war which the cultural revolutionary mood seemed ready for, but which the world balance of power did not permit China to wage. The Soviet embassy in Peking was beseiged for several weeks in January and again in May and August by great mobs of Red Guards and others. But the Chinese were unable, or did not dare, to sack and burn it as they did the British embassy on 22 August—perhaps as a surrogate. This last took place during the brief period from 19 to 23 August when the ultra-left had seized control of the Chinese Foreign Ministry.

The Soviet government reacted to all this with a basic calm. Kosygin, whilst on a visit to Britain and France in February 1967, criticised Mao openly in public speeches, virtually calling for his overthrow in one made in France. But it was noticeable that such speeches were not made on Soviet soil, and in the main Moscow's policy seemed one of waiting for the Chinese internal situation to sort itself out, although the aged Wang Ming was brought out of retirement to make some publication. A number of minor agreements between the two countries were cancelled unilaterally that year, however, and sessions of the joint navigation commission were disrupted. Soviet defences in Siberia continued to be strengthened and plans for its economic development stepped up.

On 1 July 1968 the United States and the Soviet Union signed a draft non-proliferation treaty for nuclear weapons. China was isolated: very few major non-Communist countries yet recognised it, the main Communist parties of Asia had been seriously alienated by its policies and some 30 governments had been affected in various degrees by Red Guard attacks on their diplomatic personnel in Peking or attacks launched from Chinese embassies in their capitals during the period when cultural revolutionaries dominated China's foreign policy. Of Communist parties, only the Burmese White Flags, the Malaysian, Philippine, Thai, Netherlands and New Zealand remained pro-Chinese. Elsewhere only fractions and splinter groups continued to back Peking. Nyerere of Tanzania was almost a lone supporter amongst governments, because China had started to fulfil its undertaking to build the strategic railway, providing Tanzania with US$400 million, and to train the Tanzanian armed forces. The Soviet Union by contrast now had diplomatic relations with most countries in the world, including all the Southeast Asian ones except the Philippines, as well as detente with America. Even Japan had begun to thaw towards it a little, although Taiwan did not change its attitude. In the Middle East and South Asia the Soviet Union wielded considerable influence and its position in Eastern Europe was also improved despite the impending Czech crisis; in the background, its armed strength continued to expand.

By mid-1968 the Cultural Revolution had largely spent itself, and order was being restored in China by the army. Liu and his followers had been toppled, and the educational system revamped to produce politically reliable people rather than highly skilled specialists. Modernisation and the pursuit of higher learning had been set back many years, but a positive achievement was seen in the rapid extension of primary and lower secondary education and basic medical services to cover the needs of the whole population, which hitherto had not been fully met in these respects.

The Soviet invasion of Czechoslovakia to crush the liberal party movement there and the Brezhnev doctrine of proletarian internationalism — the right of one socialist country (i.e. the Soviet Union) to intervene in other socialist countries, — pronounced on 13 November 1968 after the invasion, was perceived as an alarming portent by China, despite its dislike of the Czech liberals. Another disturbing straw in the wind for China was the Soviet-Japanese agreement for joint forest resource development projects in Siberia, signed in August. These factors, together with the shattered state of their country after the Cultural Revolution, prompted the Chinese leadership to begin trying to make serious political contact with the United States. It was to take three years of effort to achieve this, partly owing to initial opposition from Mao and/or his new chosen heir Lin Biao. But Sino-American ambassadorial talks were re-opened in Warsaw in February 1969.

All this happened whilst incidents continued to take place along the borders, about which no very informed treatment has been published so far. (Frontier matters have always been regarded as top secret in both the Communist and traditional Russian and Chinese states, to the extent that, as may be recalled from Chapter Eight, even in the very late Qing and tsarist period of 1910-11 negotiations and demarcations on the Argun river border in Northwest Manchuria were more or less successfully kept hidden from the foreign diplomatic communities.) It seems to be agreed that many of these frontier incidents were started by the Chinese during a period in the Cultural Revolution, others were no doubt incurred through movement of minority peoples in Xinjiang, and many may have been the product of sheer misunderstanding due to the lack of any proper modern delimitation and changing natural features, such as the course of the thalweg in the Manchurian boundary rivers. On the whole, because of the cautious nature of the Brezhnev foreign policy, it might be surmised that the Russians were not likely to have been responsible for any systematic border provocation, except possibly at certain strategic points and at certain times such as February 1967 or in connection with the flight of refugees from Xinjiang.

A deal of debate arose abroad as to the causes of the fighting on 2 March 1969 over the island in the Ussuri called Zhen Bao (Precious Treasure) by the Chinese and by the Russians Damanskii (a surname), which each side accused the other of starting. According to a widely accepted interpretation, the incident was probably staged by the Chinese or first deliberately publicised by them, if in fact the Russians were responsible. There appears no doubt that the Soviet army counter-attacked with overwhelming force on 15 March. Both sides played up the tension violently, obviously for internal consumption as well as to discredit the other in the eyes of the world. Both might have been using the incident to prepare their people for closer relations with America. The machinations for power of Lin Biao have also been cited as a possible cause, for he acquired much prominence as a result of the Chinese military response, emerging at the Ninth Congress of the Chinese Communist Party as Mao's acknowledged heir. Yet despite the bellicose talk there seemed no real desire for war by either country, and Moscow soon began to call for talks with Peking, setting successive deadlines which the latter ignored without however making any serious steps towards hostilities.

The Russians accompanied their demand for negotiations with other moves. The number of Soviet divisions on the frontier with China was raised to 21, and China rapidly built up its border forces as well. The main Soviet policy initiatives in Asia that year were certainly directed against China, though unsuccessful. A conference of world Communist parties in Moscow in June failed by far to secure a unanimous condemnation of China, nor did the Asian Collective Security Plan mooted by Brezhnev in the same month meet with much response from governments. Soviet feelers to Taiwan were rebuffed, despite the improvement in relations with Japan. Then at the end of the summer Moscow began to assume a more threatening stance. On 28 August the Soviet deputy defence minister stated in an article in *Pravda* that any war between his country and China would certainly involve the use of nuclear weapons. Soviet diplomats sounded out the United

States, Eastern European countries and pro-Soviet Communist parties as to how they would view a Soviet attack on China. Yet the reactions were generally unenthusiastic, and the whole exercise might have been undertaken mainly to alarm the Chinese.

It may indeed have had this effect, for Zhou Enlai met with Kosygin in Peking on 11 September and, despite making pre-conditions about the agenda on 18 September, on 7 October 1969 China agreed to open border talks with no demands for territory on its part and a guarantee of the *status quo* with no use of force even if the talks failed. This marked the beginning of a new phase in the history of relations between the two countries, which continued until about 1982.

13 1969-1978:

WORLD-WIDE RIVALRY DURING THE SINO-AMERICAN AND SOVIET-AMERICAN DETENTES

From this point any discussion of Sino-Soviet relations is meaningless in isolation from a consideration of the general tenor of world events and the relations of both countries with the United States, Japan and Western Europe. Of the greatest importance were their relations with the United States. Starting from 1969, Beijing* began to effect a radical re-alignment of its foreign policy designed to seek world recognition as a great power and obtain Western technological, diplomatic and financial support to counter the powerful threat it perceived from Moscow. After the United States invaded Cambodia in March 1970 the Sino-American ambassadorial talks were again suspended, but when Mao's old friend, the left-wing American journalist Edgar Snow, visited him at the end of the year, China's new foreign policy course appears already to have been set. In April 1971 a US table-tennis team went to China, and in July US Secretary of State Kissinger flew secretly to Beijing to arrange for the visit of President Nixon. The policy of detente with the United States, favoured especially by Zhou Enlai within the Chinese leadership, was being challenged by Lin Biao, who saw himself gradually losing favour to Zhou in Mao's sight. Lin had apparently long maintained some secret contacts of an insurance nature with the Soviet Union and in September 1971, possibly with Soviet support, he attempted a military coup against Mao and his supporters. When it failed, Lin seemingly fled towards the Soviet frontier in an aircraft which crashed in Outer Mongolia on 13 September, killing all on board. The still mysterious incident cleared the way for the denouement of the Sino-American entente. Nixon's visit took place early in 1972, followed by the

* By the wish of the Chinese government, Peking is now known as Beijing in official and international usage.

141

Shanghai Communique announcing the new *rapprochement*.
China had ceased to be an isolated revolutionary state or a Soviet
semi-satellite, but was emerging onto the stage of world politics as
an important independent actor, although for the next decade
showing signs that it found the environment still somewhat
strange.

Even before this dramatic event the entire world balance of
power had begun to shift. Developments of far-reaching
significance became apparent in Europe in 1969 and 1970. By
this time West German industry had reached the position of
continental dominance it would have attained much earlier if two
world wars had not been fought to prevent it. In February 1969
the Soviet Union and West Germany signed an agreement
whereby the latter was to supply a large-diameter pipeline for the
transmission of natural gas from Siberia to Central Europe, and
on 12 August 1970 the Treaty of Moscow was concluded between
these two states. Through this West Germany recognised the
Oder-Neisse river frontier established by Stalin between Poland
and East Germany, thus acquiescing at last to the retention by
Poland of the substantial territories that it had acquired from
Hitler's Germany. With this treaty and others recently concluded
between West Germany and the East European Communist
countries, a measure of reconciliation to the bitter legacy of the
Second World War in Europe was achieved, and the way to some
extent paved for a resumption of the close diplomatic and
economic ties which had existed between Germany and both
tsarist and Soviet Russia for most of the period between 1815 and
1941. The gas pipeline deal bade fair to place the recipients of the
gas (which included West Germany, Italy and France) in partial
dependence on the Soviet fuel supplied, simultaneously
promoting a Soviet direction to the exports of West Germany's
powerful industry. From 1970 then, a renewed German-Russian
alliance and a Soviet economic domination of Western Europe
emerged as shadowy future possibilities. For the present however,
these were far off and the huge dimensions of the gas project
meant that it would take some fifteen years to realise.

The early years of the new decade were ones of false optimism
for the Western Alliance, after over two decades of unbroken
prosperity. Far from West Germany being drawn into the Soviet
orbit, a united non-Communist Europe seemed to be emerging.
The political demise and death of de Gaulle had removed the

most implacable brake on the European Economic Community (EEC), which Britain, Ireland and Denmark joined in January 1973. France had undergone a second industrial revolution since the Second World War which brought it to a position not far behind Germany, and with these two as a nucleus the EEC looked ready to become a new super-power in its own right.

Meanwhile the Soviet Union had by 1969 achieved a rough parity with the United States in nuclear weapons and felt able to negotiate from a position of strength. Consequently, as the Chinese-US *rapprochment* and the burgeoning of the EEC took shape, Moscow under Brezhnev became ever more positive in its efforts to establish a closer relationship with the United States. These were prompted not only by a wish to parry the Chinese, but by a desire for easier access to American high technology and grain supplies and a lessening of the armaments' burden, in order to meet pressing expectations of the Soviet public for better living and to remedy the now apparent Soviet backwardness in some of the most advanced sectors such as computers. The increasingly obvious defeat of the United States in Vietnam, with all the attendant obloquy heaped on it at home and abroad, impelled Washington in the same direction of detente. Tension between the super-powers, already much less than in Stalin's time, relaxed remarkably.

The first round of the Strategic Arms Limitation Talks (SALT) was held in November–December 1969. A treaty on the exploitation of minerals in the sea-bed was concluded between the United States, the Soviet Union and Britain in February 1971, and a compromise quadrupartite agreement on Berlin on 3 September. The second round of the SALT talks in November 1972 produced an agreement sanctioning a superiority in Soviet ICBMs and did not cover weapons in which the United States was superior: notably the strategic bombers and the US carrier, foreign-based strike aircraft and the MIRVs. But after the SALT treaty, both super-powers continued building new types of armaments on which no restrictions had been placed.

In 1973 the Americans at last extricated themselves from the disastrous war in Vietnam. The United States now stood weakened, its hitherto invincible military reputation tarnished and a new mood of isolationism overtaking its people. Billions of dollars had been wasted that might have re-equipped its industry, the older sections of which were now beginning to sink into obsolescence. But the United States was still keeping a lead in high technology, in which it began catering to the demands of the Communist states whose appetites appeared almost insatiable. With a mutually hostile Moscow and Beijing both seeking American grain and know-how, the United States was in a very favourable position. Nixon held a summit with Mao in Beijing in February 1972 and another with Brezhnev in Moscow in May 1973. Brezhnev visited the United States and addressed Congress in June of that year. Nixon again went to Moscow in June 1974, and Nixon's successor Ford went so far as to disturb the Chinese by having his summit with Brezhnev at Vladivostok at the end of 1974. Yet detente with China continued, the United States having helped it to gain a seat on the UN Security Council in 1972.

America's diplomatic successes of this period veiled the fact that its power had reached a turning-point and begun somewhat to decline relative to the other contenders for world influence. After the fall of Nixon by reason of the Watergate scandal in 1973, Gerald Ford succeeded as the first of a series of less able presidents who compounded their country's difficulties through clumsy foreign policies. Under the incumbency of Carter from 1976 new tension was introduced into America's relations with Moscow by his verbal espousal of the cause of civil rights throughout the world and employment of a strongly anti-Soviet foreign policy adviser of Polish descent, Brzezinski. The US administration became more suspicious of Soviet intentions.

Japanese GNP and technology had already begun to catch up with those of the world leaders in the 1970s. Having opted by national consensus not to re-arm after the Second World War, the Japanese alone of all major nations were left free to spend all their resources on economic development. They relied on the US nuclear umbrella for their defence, at the same time assuming a basically harmless posture towards China and the Soviet Union by having minimum overt military ties with America. The result, in the hands of a brilliant industrial leadership, was the rise of Japan's GNP to a position rivalling that of the Soviet Union by 1981, whilst Japanese technology in many fields surpassed Soviet.

Moreover, Japan weathered the great economic storms which now began to buffet the world better than most Western countries. Late in 1973 OPEC (Organization of Petroleum Exporting Countries) started a series of increases in oil prices, thereby launching a massive inflation affecting the whole of the capitalist world and also the Communist countries in measure as they were involved in international trade. The economies of the Western nations, in many cases already running on a heavy fiscal deficit, received a severe blow. Decline set in particularly precipitately in Britain, which behind the blaze of postwar prosperity had long been suffering from short-sighted leadership, ageing industry, an archaic trade union system, and a kind of muted cricket-game civil war between socialism and capitalism. Inflation mounted everywhere with the passing of the 1970s, causing the movement towards Western European unity to become more and more bogged down in economic problems. But Japan was less affected than almost any other capitalist state.

Changes within China meanwhile facilitated its entry into the nexus of ties involved in great-power status. As Mao became more aged and inconsequential, succession groups contended. During the early 1970s the leadership group advocating modernisation met with strong opposition from the radicals (the so-called Gang of Four) headed by Mao's wife, Jiang Qing, who believed China must stay aloof from capitalism and the Soviet Union alike in order to preserve the gains of the revolution and maintain national unity. But Deng Xiaoping, the new strongman of the modernisation group, had become vice-chairman of the Chinese Communist Party, vice-premier and chief of staff by January 1975, gradually taking over the role of the now fatally ill Zhou Enlai, who died early in 1976. As soon as Mao died in the following September, the light weight of the radical leaders was exposed and they were quickly overthrown by a coalition of opponents to the right. The death of Mao heralded a new stage in the Chinese revolution, that may be compared in some ways with that which followed the death of Stalin in Russia, or Thermidor in the French revolution. Hua Guofeng, appointed chairman on Mao's death, occupied a position somewhat intermediary between the radicals and Deng, but the latter's influence increased rapidly. Thus from the fall of the Gang of Four Chinese government policies increasingly began to stress pragmatism and modernisation.

Against the background of this rough sketch of the main trends of power politics, let us now look closer at Sino-Soviet relations in this period. These were characterised on the one hand by an extraordinary stalemate in direct dealings, on the other by tremendous activity on the part of each to contain the other.

Their counter-manoeuvres reached into many parts of the world.

China's whole strategy against Moscow was based on using the West and Japan to bottle up Soviet might, with a secondary drive to win greater influence in the Third World, mainly in Africa. Ever since Zhou Enlai's report to the Tenth Congress of the CCP in August 1973 it was a cardinal foreign policy tenet of Beijing that the main threat from the Soviet Union was to the West. Moscow, it was maintained, was 'making a feint in the East to attack the West'. In fact about two-thirds of the Soviet armed forces were, and remain, deployed against Europe, but the interpretation placed on this by Beijing was designed first and foremost to further China's diplomatic interests, which lay in fuelling Western hostility to the Soviet Union. China recognised the EEC in 1975. Chinese spokesmen tried to encourage the wavering progress of Western European unity, and began to back the various Western measures to combat Soviet activities in Africa and the Middle East, stressing the threat which these latter posed.

China's trade and ties with the various Western countries increased (although not fulfilling the exaggerated hopes in some Western business quarters), and a growing number of contracts were signed with Western firms for the supply and installation of equipment on credit. In this period neither China nor any Western country was willing to enter into any close political or military alignment, in fact the diplomatic relations between Washington and Beijing remained officially — though not *de facto* — on a liaison office level. Yet the general tendency between 1969 and 1978 was for ties between China and the West to strengthen gradually, whilst Sino-Japanese relations thawed.

Soviet global strategy against China consisted in a more emphatic pursuit of its previous course of containment and seeking to re-establish a working relationship with Beijing. China's greater success with the industrialised countries was counterbalanced by greater Soviet success in the Third World, especially in Asia, where Moscow's steadily growing military and economic resources were a telling argument in its favour despite a gradual slight slowing-down in its GNP growth.

Over this period the ideological dispute lessened and changed. In November 1970 China extended its concept of peaceful co-existence to relations between all states, not only between socialist and capitalist, a principle entirely at odds with the 1969 Brezhnev doctrine of proletarian internationalism to which the Soviet

Union adhered throughout the 1970s. Sino-Soviet competition for the allegiance of Communist parties slowly dwindled in these years. Most parties had either opted definitely for one side or the other, split or become neutral, and the Communist ideological world seemed to have finally fallen apart after the last international meeting of Communist parties in Moscow in 1976. In the Third World the jealousy of the two countries took on new aspects. From 1969, and still more from 1971, China like the Soviet Union in the 1950s gradually attempted to normalise its relations with many Asian and African states and increase its trade and aid to them. After the fall of the Gang of Four in 1976 China reduced or ended its encouragement to the various revolutionary groups in the Third World.

Africa remained one of the foci of change and international competition, forming one of the chief fields of Sino-Soviet Third World rivalry. Between 1970 and 1977 China offered aid to 29 African countries against 22 supplied by the Russians, and its economic aid to Africa amounted to twice that of the Soviet Union. China's trade with Africa was likewise greater than that of the Russians, Chinese exports to that continent in particular being some two-thirds larger than Soviet by 1978. But the Soviet Union furnished arms to 21 African countries as well as two liberation movements (ANC in South Africa and SWAPO in Namibia), as against Chinese shipments to seventeen by about 1979. In some cases both Moscow and Beijing supplied arms to the same country at the same time. Moreover the Soviet Union got the better of China in Angola, Mozambique and the Horn of Africa, where it found a new ally in the military rulers of Ethiopia, a more important key stronghold than Somalia from which its advisers and service personnel were ejected in 1977. In Southern Africa China and the Soviet Union at first competed for influence over the revolutionary liberation groups (SWAPO in Namibia, Mugabe's ZANU in Zimbabwe, FRELIMO in Mozambique, and Neto's MPLA and Roberto's FNLA in Angola), but China gradually disengaged. According to one of the few Western scholars of Sino-Soviet relations in Africa, the Chinese advisers held their own with the Soviet ones in African estimation.

During this period the Middle East was not a major field of Sino-Soviet clashes. Soviet interest in the region was intense, concentrated on ousting the US presence and acquiring paramountcy. By contrast China's trade with and concern over the

Middle East was minor—with the exception of the People's Democratic Republic of Yemen (PDRY: Aden) but even this waned by 1978. China backed Sadat's peace endeavours with Israel and the other pro-American moves in the region, although without any special economic contribution, nor did it show much warmth towards Israel. It established relations with the conservative governments of the Persian Gulf zone—Iran and Kuwait—in 1971, and in 1972 dropped its support for the Oman Popular Front (Dhufar rebellion), which Moscow then picked up. The PDRY (Aden), South Yemen and Iraq also moved closer to Moscow, although Soviet influence was well established only in the PDRY. To the Russians, as to the British earlier, the Red Sea was important in the imperial maritime role which Moscow began to enact increasingly after the ebbing of British power east of Suez from 1956 and its final renunciation by London in 1968. Other liberation movements backed by the Chinese which they also abandoned in this period were the South Yemen, Eritrean and Somali, whilst the Russians emerged more and more as a major power in the Middle East until dealt a strong blow when Egypt broke with them in 1976 and the Israeli-Egyptian peace negotiations started.

In the Indian sub-continent China continued to back Pakistan and the Soviet Union India. India with Soviet approval triumphed over Pakistan in the war of December 1971, from which arose the new state of Bangladesh. This latter followed a slightly pro-Chinese orientation for some years as a safeguard against India, yet the Soviet Union supplied over four times more aid to it than did China. China's aid to Pakistan stopped well short of a friendship treaty of the kind binding India and the Soviet Union since August 1971 (the Twenty-year Friendship Treaty). Pakistan even received about one-third more aid from Moscow than from Beijing. Only Nepal and Sri Lanka received more aid from China than from the Russians, and Sri Lanka also did far more trade with China than with the Soviet Union. Soviet aid to India continued to be substantial; the Indian armed forces were heavily dependent on Soviet equipment and the Russians were India's second largest trading partner. But India's dependence on Soviet economic aid somewhat lessened with the growth of its own heavy industry and the knowledge that the Soviet economy itself required inputs of high technology from the United States and Japan. Although the Sino-Indian border dispute remained unsettled it was quiescent, and India no less than Pakistan wanted to limit Soviet influence. As a result, the relations of the two South Asian powers improved somewhat. Ambassadors were exchanged in 1976 for the first time since the early 1960s, and progress was made towards settling their differences on a bilateral basis. Moreover during this period neither of the Communist powers could match the US$25 billion worth of aid extended by the Western nations, with whom all the South Asian nations also did more trade.

Southeast Asia is an area of historical links with China, within whose possible future sphere of influence it lies. Most countries in the region have substantial Chinese minorities which have long controlled much of their trade and commerce. Malaysia's population is nearly 50 per cent Chinese. Consequently, the indigenous Southeast Asians have for several generations feared the Chinese, and much of their modern policy has been directed to combating them. The alignment of all the Southeast Asian states apart from Vietnam has been essentially independent or pro-American since 1969, and they have maintained normal relations with both Moscow and Beijing only so as to stay out of the toils of either. In Vietnamese eyes, China posed an especial threat, deep-rooted because of the 1000 year domination of Annam by China from 196 BC to 939 AD and later Chinese attempts to regain it. Once the American threat in Vietnam was eliminated by the victory of the north over the south in 1975, it was natural that the Vietnamese inclined to look to the Russians for protection from any possible danger from China. A Soviet-Vietnamese alliance was eventually to materialise through China's opposition to Hanoi's invasion of Kampuchea (Cambodia), following the establishment of the ferocious nativist Pol Pot Communist regime there in 1976, which China backed. It may be noted that China's support for insurgencies in Southeast Asia—notably the Thai and Malaysian Communists—however limited, continued throughout this period despite its dropping of many liberation fronts in Africa and the Middle East. In 1978 therefore the Soviet Union was predominent in Vietnam, Kampuchea torn by strife between the Pol Pot forces and the Vietnamese invasion force, and the rest of the region virtually outside either Soviet or Chinese influence.

During the 1970s the Soviet position in the whole of East Asia remained checked. Taiwan turned a cold shoulder as before and

China was much more successful with Japan, for despite the terrible events of the Sino-Japanese war and their different development the two countries shared a fundamental cultural heritage going back over 4000 years. The Russians and the Japanese had been in contact only since the mid-nineteenth century. A bad Russian image had predominated in Japan from as far back as 1895, reinforced in the largely conservative Japanese political spectrum by the Bolshevik revolution and Communist rule in Russia. Japan's loss of the Kuriles and South Sakhalin to the Soviet Union in 1945 furthered this. Moscow refused to sign the Japanese peace treaty in 1952. A Soviet-Japanese treaty of 1956 renewed diplomatic and trade ties, but did not touch the island problem. Japan now began to demand the return of the Southern Kuriles and the Soviet Union agreed to this, but changed its mind again in 1960. A very conciliatory Soviet attitude to Japan in 1971 hardened again the next year upon the normalisation of Japan's ties with China and the latter's espousal of Japan's island cause. Beijing began more actively seeking to win over Japan in negotiations begun in 1975 to produce a peace and friendship treaty, and Japanese businessmen returned eagerly to China. Not all the Soviet need for Japanese investment in Eastern Siberia could outweigh the fundamental mutual suspicion of Tokyo and Moscow, which remained obvious despite improvement in trade and cultural ties and a limited Japanese involvement in Siberian development.

As for Korea, it stayed set in its previous mould, with the south as an American satellite having no diplomatic relations with Moscow, and the north maintaining a fundamental independence through careful balancing between its two powerful Communist neighbours. Chinese influence in Pyongyang was somewhat greater than Russian after 1971, but Beijing no more than Moscow was really able to control Kim Ilsung.

Whilst the action in Sino-Soviet relations in these nine years took place mainly on the global diplomatic scale (with the possible exception of the Lin Biao or other clandestine affairs in China), direct relations stayed almost at a standstill, effectively stymied at all stages by China. Before the border talks opened on 20 October 1969 the Chinese government had insisted, as mentioned at the end of Chapter Twelve, that certain agenda items would have to be dealt with satisfactorily before the talks *per se* could commence. The first of these items was that all military forces should be withdrawn from all disputed territories in the border zone. Since these disputed territories lay within the Soviet frontiers, being those on which the two sides' representatives had disagreed in the February 1964 consultations, a troop withdrawal would have been a unilateral one by the Soviet Union. Whatever the other prerequiste Chinese agenda items may have been, this alone sufficed to prevent any real progress. At no time in this period did the Soviet government see the advisability of taking such a step.

Why therefore did the Chinese insist upon it? One convincing explanation is that they were reluctant to yield an inch of favour to the Soviet government at a time when China was still so backward in modern technology and especially subject to factionalism in its ruling circles during the declining years of Mao and following his death. Although outside observers have differed in their evaluation of the activities of the various disgraced Chinese leaders who were suspected of pro-Soviet affiliations (Gao Gang, Peng Dehuai and last but not least Lin Biao), there is every reason to believe that the Chinese ruling circles' fear of Soviet penetration into their politics was well founded. A further explanation can be found in Beijing's wish to assure the West and Japan of its reliability as a diplomatic partner and field of investment, at least until such time as China could be as well integrated with the world capitalist scene as it wished.

Faced with this unremitting Chinese hostility, the Soviet government made use of the talks to offer a wide range of minor concessions, which if accepted would counter American moves towards Beijing and lead to a better climate of Sino-Soviet relations and if rejected would serve a useful propaganda purpose to impress domestic and international opinion and possibly any Chinese who might rise to the fore to oppose the anti-Soviet line.

At the first session of the border talks from October to December 1969 the Soviet side proposed discussion of all differences, leaving the vexed border issue until the atmosphere was better. Many new offers were added by the Russians during the further sessions which took place throughout 1970 and from mid-January 1971 to the summer. On 15 January 1971 Moscow profferred a new non-aggression treaty or a reaffirmation of the 1950 treaty, and also accepted the thalweg as the frontier in navigable rivers and the mid-channel in non-navigable ones. It expressed its willingness to hand over to China certain islands in the Ussuri including Zhenbao, but not the disputed Black Bear Island close to Khabarovsk. None of this was acceptable to the Chinese, who now averred that all that was required was an intermediate agreement on maintaining the *status quo* on the borders, and finally prevented even this by demanding again that Moscow accept their concept of disputed areas.

On 20 March 1972 the Soviet negotiator Ilychev returned to Beijing to re-open the talks bearing an important new concession: namely Moscow's willingness to establish relations with China on the basis of the five principles of peaceful co-existence, thus accepting the Chinese ideological stance enunciated in November 1970. This was clearly aimed to achieve some results between Nixon's February 1972 visit to Beijing and his projected May visit to Moscow, leaving Brezhnev one way or the other more certain as to the best line he should take with Nixon. Further Soviet offers to China on 14 June 1973 (the day before Brezhnev met Nixon in Washington) and 25 June 1974 (48 hours before Nixon's final visit to Moscow) were also timed to influence relations with the United States. The 1973 package included long-term expanded trade agreements, resumption of deliveries of industrial equipment to China, and scientific, medical, sports and journalist exchanges. All these gestures were rejected by the Chinese because at no time during the three-year negotiations did the Soviet side consent to pull back its forces in the border regions, which it reinforced to a total of 42 divisions in 1972 and 46 by 1978 according to some estimates. Efforts were made to build up Soviet basic strength in East Asia by great investment in Siberia, and the construction of a second main-line railway from the Urals to the Pacific (the Baikal-Amur Mainline) was begun in 1974 at an estimated total cost of up to US$15 billion.

The Tenth Congress of the CCP in the late summer of 1973 indicated such rigidity in the Chinese stand that negotiations languished and seem to have stopped in the autumn of 1974. Then on 27 December 1975 a sudden conciliatory move was made by the Chinese in the release of the imprisoned crew of a Soviet helicopter which had violated their frontier in March 1974. This release was accompanied by renewed Chinese propaganda blasts against the Soviet Union, causing skilled observers to connect the two events with an intricate scenario of in-fighting in Beijing. Moscow declined to make any fresh offers in default of a more unambiguous indication of China's wish for better relations.

Mao's death was greeted in Moscow with an almost total cessation of polemics against China, and the return of Ilychev to the negotiating table in Beijing on 27 November 1976, but thereafter the talks were again suspended at an uncertain date. A resumption of attacks on China in the Soviet media occurred in the spring of 1977, but on 24 February 1978 the USSR once more called for 'a joint statement of the principles of mutual relations'. China's rejection of this was followed by a thirteen-day tour of inspection of the frontier defences by Brezhnev. Thus 1978 opened with continuing stalemate, China being held in partial military encirclement between Vietnam and the Soviet divisions on the frontier, but holding its own with the Russians on the world scale.

14 Since 1978:

TOWARDS NEW BALANCES OF
POWER

The year 1978 marked an important turning point in international relations, for a series of events combined suddenly to throw the United States and the Soviet Union into a new phase of hostility, towards which they had been drifting for the previous two years.

In April 1978 the first pro-Soviet coup took place in Afghanistan, at a time when the movement against the Shah in Iran was gradually gathering momentum and when the ineptitude of the Carter administration had already become well apparent. The developments in Afghanistan can probably be seen as an offensive-defensive move by the Russians, aimed both to head off the spread of unrest from Iran further towards their own Central Asian frontiers and to extend their presence towards the Persian Gulf, in order to escape encirclement by the combined forces of China and the West. A move towards the Persian Gulf, as to the Red Sea, was in the historic Russian tradition to advance towards warm-water ports and unrestricted access to the oceans. Down the centuries it appears to have appealed as a long-term possibility to generations of leaders in Moscow.

The establishment of a pro-Moscow government in Kabul naturally disturbed the Chinese and Western governments and may have been a factor in the successful conclusion of the three-year negotiations for the Sino-Japanese friendship treaty in August — an event of even greater ultimate portent than the West German treaties with the Soviet Union and its Eastern European allies had been. It included a clause committing both signatories to combat 'hegemonism' — the current Chinese ideological code word for the extension of Soviet power. The Sino-Japanese treaty produced a reaction of alarm in Moscow, just as Afghanistan had in the other side, precipitating the signing of the Soviet-Vietnamese and Soviet-Afghan friendship treaties in October.

The Vietnamese treaty in particular then prompted Peking into fully normalising its relations with the United States on 15 December, and into launching a seventeen-day war of indecisive outcome against Vietnam in January 1979. Within about nine months the power alignment had thus hardened to a marked degree.

Moscow derived considerable propaganda benefit from the US entanglement with the revolution in Iran, which had finally broken out violently in October 1978, culminating in the fall of the Shah in January 1979 and the surrender of his army on 11 February. As a previous staunch backer of the monarch, the United States now found itself the target of the pent-up resentments of the Islamic revolutionaries, and to the chagrin of its well-wishers provided the world with a spectacle of impotence over the much publicised arrest of the staff of its Teheran embassy and the fiasco of the attempted military rescue.

In an atmosphere of unease Brezhnev and Carter at last met in Vienna for their first and only summit in June 1979, to sign the second SALT treaty, despite strong opposition to it in the US Senate. Before it could be ratified, a Muslim nationalist insurgency against the new Afghan regime and the unedifying in-fighting amongst the pro-Moscow Afghans (both with ramifications threatening to extend into Soviet Central Asia) induced Brezhnev to send the Soviet army into Afghanistan in December 1979. This doomed SALT II to rejection by the US Senate—although it has apparently been observed by the two sides none the less—and created dismay around the world assiduously fanned by Western and Chinese propagandists, glad to have a distraction from Iran.

Ronald Reagan's election as president in November 1980 on a platform of massive re-armament and resistance to the Soviet Union, combined with strongly conservative domestic policies, further worsened Soviet-American relations. The days of personal summitry seemed over and a new cold war to be under way.

But this ran counter to the basic strategic aspirations of Brezhnev, who had kept detente as a key aim whilst pressing on with Soviet arms-building and seeing no need to withdraw Soviet power back into the carapace of the Soviet bloc, as the American hawks would have liked. Now in his declining years, he studiously avoided all dangerous conflicts with the United States. Caution was forced on him the more because the Afghan insurgents developed a strong resistance to the Soviet invaders, who became entangled in an almost Vietnam situation. With aid supplied by Western intelligence organisations and private traders via devious routes, the guerrillas have remained effective until the present writing nearly four years later. On top of this, a well-organised revolt by the Polish workers against the Communist regime in their country began in 1980, so that the Moscow government felt beleaguered on several sides.

It appears that Brezhnev clung on to power in the Kremlin long after he was capable of exercising it fully—a circumstance at which those who were engaged in the struggle for his seat perhaps connived. The contest for the succession was evidently concluded before he died, although he retained authority in foreign affairs until the end. Brezhnev's last decade was marked by the massive growth of the black sector of the Soviet economy and general corruption, associated with a gradual slow-down in GNP growth. This amounted to only 2.1 per cent in 1979 according to an American academic estimate, and to less than 2 per cent in 1982. The official growth target for 1983 is 3.2 per cent. The Soviet economy remained powerful but faced deep-seated problems of planning and operational effectiveness, coupled with the long-term prospect of labour shortages due to falling birthrates in the European-populated main industrial areas. It suffered deplorable harvests in 1979 and 1980, and meanwhile debates were taking place over investment allocation for the eleventh Five Year Plan. In this condition the Soviet government could not eagerly either meet or decline the challenge of a stepped-up arms race from America.

The above factors provide an explanation for the atrophy becoming visible in Soviet foreign policy from 1980, which enabled the Americans, once their Iranian embarassment had been resolved, to reassert themselves by 1982 as the paramount power in the Middle East, and less decisively in the Third World generally. Yet the Middle East remained inherently most unstable, offering promising future opportunities for the Soviet Union. Nor were the Americans able to eliminate Soviet influence in Syria, the PDYR, Ethiopia, Mozambique and Angola, still less in Cuba, nor to prevent the waxing presence of the Soviet navy in the world's oceans and the strengthening of Moscow's ties with Vietnam, which gave the Russians the use of important naval and air bases, nor the unfolding of the Soviet gas pipeline schemes into Western Europe. Still less could Washington do anything effective in 1982 to prevent the infliction of martial law on Poland, where the security troops were able more or less to impose Moscow's will on a sullen nation.

From 1978, as Soviet-US relations deteriorated, China drew closer not only to the United States but to the whole world capitalist system, closer than the Soviet Union had ever been at the height of detente. In 1980 the Beijing government joined the World Bank — which the Soviet Union has never done — and by that year over 2400 Sino-foreign contracts had been signed at provincial levels. Overseas Chinese were particularly active at promoting joint ventures with the Chinese state economic organisations, and multiple contacts developed with Western countries and Japan. On the domestic front there was a pronounced right-ward swing. By 1980 Deng Xiaoping emerged as supreme, with the replacement of Hua Guofeng by Zhao Ziyang as prime minister. Deng abandoned most of Maoism, going all out for modernisation, steering an economic course well to the right of that followed in the Soviet Union, and a political course similar to the Soviet one. The activities of the security police were curbed and the system of public indoctrination campaigns was ended. Profitability, competition and moderate consumerism were encouraged, hundreds of thousands of tourists were let into the country, and some freedom was permitted to religious believers and intellectuals. Small private businesses were permitted in cities. More fundamental was the amazing alteration in policy to the peasants. A series of changes in the laws relating to the organisation of land cultivation in the communes was completed in 1980. Responsibility for cultivation and considerably greater opportunities for profit-making were conferred on peasant teams or individual families in a wide range of different organisational options. This was a radical departure from the Maoist system, and much more flexible than the method followed in the Soviet Union.

The Chinese economy throve well in the new atmosphere despite numerous growing pains, for GNP rose by an average of 9 per cent per annum from 1976 to 1981. Thus far Deng's strategy has succeeded, at the same time paying a price in risk to the stability of the Communist system and in the increase of US influence over Beijing's foreign policy.

So diplomatic events in the years 1980–82 seemed to be shaping rather on the model of 1890–1914, with the Soviet Union, like imperial Germany before it, a powerful, ambitious, yet politically immature central power feared and mistrusted by surrounding powers, and itself feeling the target of encirclement. In this scenario China seemed to be cast in the former role of tsarist Russia, as a needer of aid for development and a demographic make-weight for the West. Just in such circumstances had the old European alliance system been created, and the European powers taken the fatal road to the First World War.

But even as the ominous pattern of pre-1914 seemed to be reforming, from towards the end of 1981 new stresses and strains between Washington and Beijing arose from the Reagan administration's pro-Taiwan leanings, and the incompatibility of maintaining at one and the same time close relations with the West and the independent, authoritarian economic and political system in China. The Soviet invasion of Afghanistan served to push Beijing closer to the United States, but this failed to bring the benefit to China that it had perhaps hoped. Washington did not provide any very extensive military aid, and proved reluctant to relinquish its ties with Taiwan. Beijing frequently manifested its displeasure at the latter, found itself unable to make large-scale purchases of Western military hardware, and during the course of 1982 began to discourage its people from forming free friendships with Westerners and to increase censorship of literature. At the same time its attitude to Moscow gradually softened. This eventually culminated in a distinct shift in Chinese foreign policy before 1982 was out, indicating nothing less than a move to gain for China the favourable position of medial power enjoyed by America from 1971 until President Carter, and held to a lesser extent by the Soviet Union in the late 1950s.

Little progress was made in Sino-Soviet direct relations until 1982. In March 1978 China demanded a reduction in Soviet border forces to the early 1960s level. Yet there was a tendency to inch towards improvement from 1979. The annual Manchurian river nagivation commission meetings continued even during the course of the Sino-Vietnamese war. Beijing's statement in April 1979 that it was not renewing the already long-disregarded treaty of alliance with the Soviet Union served actually to clear the way for the evolution of a new relationship on a footing more acceptable to China. When in the following month Beijing ceased polemics and called for a resumption of negotiations, Moscow responded promptly. Talks did not re-open till October, but in November the Chinese government dropped its charges of revisionism against the Soviet Union, following a deliberation of the question by a conference of experts from the Chinese Academy of Social Sciences. Then the talks were once again suspended by China in January 1980 after the Soviet army had gone into Afghanistan.

As the prospects for US-Soviet agreement blackened, Brezhnev reacted more angrily towards Reagan and a note of urgency began to creep into his routine offers of friendship to China. At the Twenty-sixth Soviet Communist Party Congress in February 1981 his position was once more made clear: 'Our proposals for the normalization of relations with China remain open, and our feelings of sympathy and respect for the Chinese people have not changed'. Beijing went on fobbing off the re-opening of negotiations, but through 1981 began gradually to allow exchange visits of small groups of language specialists, scientists, sportsmen and so on with the Soviet Union.

China was warming towards the Russians at a cautious pace, with back-steps from time to time, presumably connected to its relations with the United States and the progress of its domestic affairs. On 25 September Moscow proposed resuming border negotiations and on 16 December suggested regular scientific and technological exchanges. A rejection of these Soviet overtures on 25 December was followed on 8 January 1982 by Beijing's announcement that it made no pre-conditions for the recommencement of talks with Moscow, although the Afghan, Vietnam, border and troop problems would have to be discussed. The director of the Soviet Academy of Foreign Affairs, S. Tikhvinskii, was allowed to meet senior officials in Beijing in January. A Soviet note of 3 February asking for talks to begin and another overture from Soviet Prime Minister Tikhonov on 16 February was followed by the conclusion of an agreement providing for the re-establishment of trade over the Manchurian rivers, including trans-border container shipping. But this was not fast enough for Brezhnev, who must have been impatient to achieve some more substantial break-through before his time was up. On 24 March he made a major speech at Tashkent in Soviet Central Asia, in which he called for an end to the twenty-year hostility from Beijing and stated that the Soviet government recognised China as a socialist state, recognised its claim to

Taiwan, and had no territorial demands on China. He offered to improve state-to-state relations, but made no such suggestion for party-to-party ones. The sincerity of this Tashkent offer has been questioned by some observers, since it included no word of reductions in the Soviet forces on the frontier with China. Perhaps, however, it is nearer the mark to view the speech as an honest one, packaged with insufficient imagination by the leader of a country heavily suspicious of the Chinese and much under the influence of military counsels. Beijing responded by indicating possible interest if the Soviet border troops were in fact reduced.

Lower-level ties continued to increase. At the end of March three Chinese economists went to Moscow and in mid-May M.S. Kapitsa, head of the Far Eastern Department of the Soviet Foreign Ministry, visited Beijing. Exchanges of athletes and others proceeded throughout the year. On 19 May there was a low-key announcement in Beijing that Soviet studies would be re-activated in China, and consultations made between Chinese and foreign scholars in the field. This indicated a wish to make good what had amounted to twenty years of dangerous neglect in this area.

It was apparent that China was re-assessing the global strength and interests of the United States, but was not engaged in any such re-appraisal of its ties with Japan, which continued to become closer. On a visit to Tokyo in May Chinese Prime Minister Zhao Ziyang indicated that both the Soviet Union and the United States could be regarded as hegemonistic, but that the former was on the attack and the latter on the defence.

However — a fact of major import — on 15 June Soviet planning methods were overwhelmingly endorsed by a week-long symposium of 50 Chinese experts, and at the end of July two top Soviet economists were reported to be in Beijing. Brezhnev on 26 September made a speech at Baku in Soviet Azerbaidjan, a rein-forcement of his Tashkent oration, in which he called for normalisation of relations with China. Next day Zhao Ziyang was repeating to Zeno Suzuki in Tokyo the same things he had said about the two super-powers in May, but from early October for a space of three weeks the Sino-Soviet consultations were held in Beijing between the Deputy Foreign Ministers Leonid Ilichyev and Qian Qichen. It was reported that China had made three conditions in order of importance for normalising relations:

withdrawal of Soviet troops from the Chinese border, of Vietnamese troops from Kampuchea, and of Soviet forces from Afghanistan. Whilst these talks were in progress, Chinese spokemen made disparaging remarks about the Soviet Union to French Communist leader Marchais and West German President Carstens.

Brezhnev's personal annoyance with Reagan's policies was revealed in his last public speech, a major one at an unusual Kremlin gathering of Soviet military leaders on 27 October, at which he also made his third overture of the year to China. At the anniversary of the Soviet November revolution the Chinese minister of culture was sent to attend the celebrations in the Soviet Beijing embassy.

Brezhnev's sudden death on 10 November brought the immediate succession of Yuri Andropov, by all accounts one of the best brains to take the helm in the Kremlin for many years, although his credentials as a man who rose to power partly through the KGB strike a chill in Western hearts. The 68-year-old Andropov apparently set a course of all-round detente abroad to provide opportunity for a clean-up of corruption and rational re-organisation of the economy. In fact, he appeared to be trying to take the wind out of China's sails by pre-empting the medial power role for his own country, a role in which China was not yet really established. Only the Reagan administration seemed to disdain the flexibility now being shown by the other two powers, and the end of 1982 saw the United States and the Soviet Union locked in hazardous arms control negotiations with each other, and in debates of equally horrendous implications within their own governments.

In the early days after Brezhnev's death the Sino-Soviet atmosphere displayed the warmth customary on the commencement of a new reign. Beijing Foreign Minister Huang Hu attended the funeral, met Gromyko and was singled out by Andropov for a long conversation. On 17 November it was announced that the talks were to resume at an unspecified date, and on 25 November Adropov spoke out for detente with China. But the usual cool breezes were not long in returning, for China sent no delegation to the Moscow ceremonies to mark the sixtieth anniversary of the 1922 Soviet federal consitution at the end of December. Yet the year ended on a slightly optimistic note, when on 31 December word was given that the consultations would recommence after the Chinese Lunar New Year, and China let it be known that it was not demanding the removal of all Soviet forces from the frontier, but simply their reduction to reasonable frontier-guard proportions.

The changed attitude of Beijing to Moscow was a part of the new Chinese foreign policy line revealed by Party leader Hu Yaobang on 4 September in a speech to the Twelfth Chinese Communist Party Congress. Under the new line China was to play a role independent of both the United States and the Soviet Union, concentrating on the Third World but not seeking leadership of it. Subsequent developments etched the contours of this plainly. For instance on 19 December a leading Chinese magazine denounced both US and Soviet hegemonism in the Third World, and Zhao Ziyang left for a tour of Egypt and Black Africa before the end of the month. At the same time it became apparent that China intended to remain tilted more to the West and above all to Japan for technological aid, whilst seeking to maintain friendly and not overly close relations with both superpowers. The present writer sensed the reality of this already in September 1982 during a tour of Northeast China, where local officials responsible for investment admitted to preferring Japanese credit at favourable 8–9 per cent interest to more expensive US loans, yet the well-preserved Soviet war memorials provided a constant reminder of aid that might be called in should China again be at risk of becoming the prey of a Western or East Asian state. The interest of the Chinese government in having a good relationship with the Soviet Union in order to help buttress its Communist political and economic structure should also not be totally dismissed as a factor underlying the foreign policy change. From the West, Beijing goes on needing technology and food imports, just as Moscow does, but neither wishes to absorb much of Western freedom along with them. It remains to be seen how soon China will fully achieve the new stance between the super-powers which it now apparently seeks.

At the present time China and Russia still present a study in contrasts, but to a more limited degree than at any previous time in their history. Moreover, the gap between them may be expected to close considerably more in the not-too-distant future.

The Soviet Union had a population of 269 million in 1982, with Russians proper (the Great Russians) making up only a bare majority (52.4 per cent in 1979). In addition, the per annum growth rate for Russians in 1979 was 0.7 per cent whilst the growth rate for the Muslim minority (the largest non-European group), was 2.47 per cent. In 1982 the population of China was 1 024 890 000 with a growth rate of 1.5–1.7 per cent and overwhelmingly composed of Han Chinese, minority groups being insignificant in comparison. Short of mass cloning, there is no way the Russian population can ever catch up with the Chinese.

In economic power, the contrast is of course in the opposite direction. According to World Bank statistics, the Soviet GNP per capita was US$4110 in 1982, whilst that of China was US$260. These figures indicate a Soviet GNP of US$1105 billion and a Chinese one of US$266.5 billion, under a quarter of the Soviet. But in the opinion of such an authority as Dwight Perkins, Harvard professor of economics and modern China studies and director of the Harvard Institute of International Development, the likelihood of China's rapid development for the rest of the century is very great. He predicts sustained growth rates of 5–9 per cent if present policies are maintained; assuming Soviet growth continues at about its present level, this should lead to China producing a GNP 86 per cent that of the Soviet Union in absolute terms within the next two decades if growth rates at the upper end of the scale are achieved, and 50 per cent that of the Soviet Union if a growth rate of 5 per cent is maintained. Even in the latter case, the balance of power between the two countries will have been substantially altered. The advantages of a huge, hard-working and modest-living population are to be seen in this situation.

In such a perspective Chinese military power could be expected to wax commensurately. Currently placed at around 7–8 per cent of GNP, its military expenditure if maintained at the same percentage over the next twenty years would produce a defence establishment of formidable size, bearing in mind that China is already the third-largest world-spender on military items. Soviet defence expenditure in recent years is reported at widely ranging figures—from 5.3 per cent of GNP (Soviet figures and *Quarterly Economic Review* 1982) to 13 per cent (CIA figures for 1979). Its expansion depends on the expansion of the total GNP, or the willingness of the Soviet population to accept restrictions on their living standard, both of which are questionable. So if today's trends continue, whether the United States and the Soviet Union continue their arms race or by some superhuman feat of rationality contrive to limit it, the Chinese can be expected to go on quietly building up their forces uninvolved in any limitation pressure.

The Soviet Union now has perhaps as many as 50 divisions stationed near the Chinese borders or in Mongolia, to a total of about 1 million men out of a total of 3 705 000 in all its armed forces. A roughly equivalent number are stationed at central strategic points in the Soviet Union, another million are deployed against NATO in the Western parts of the Union, about 600 000 are in Eastern Europe and about 100 000 in Afghanistan. The cost of maintaining the troops facing China was estimated to be about 2 per cent of GNP in 1979. China has a total armed force of about 4 million, some 3.6 million of whom are deployed in the border regions against the Soviet Union. The strain on the Beijing budget is relatively greater, but compensated for by the fact that unlike the Soviet Union China has no other major enemy of which to take account, although it does have potential sources of unrest in Xinjiang and Tibet. The nuclear power backing the Soviet forces facing China is enormously greater than that disposed of by China, as of July 1982 including some 100 of the latest SS 20 MRBMs, the first totally mobile, easily camouflageable missile. Yet the Chinese nuclear arsenal is making steady progress, and although much inferior to the Soviet in numbers and targetting accuracy can already be accounted more than a negligable deterrent.

If China strengthens, as predicted, the incentives for the Soviet government to come to terms will mount, whilst the difficulties which the Chinese government may possibly be expected to meet in controlling the expectations of its colossal population may make it more inclined to seek friendship from a country run on similar lines.

The logic of power struggle will maintain Sino-Soviet rivalry in one form or another, yet the danger of a Sino-Soviet war has been discounted by nearly all serious observers right from the start of the conflict in 1960. China will be in no position to start one for decades, and in the analysis of the present writer the international posture of the Soviet Union is still basically more defensive than offensive, its concentration of forces against Western Europe being much higher than against China and motivated in the last resort much more by internal political reasons than aggressive ones. Given that Moscow wants to outface the United States, it wants much more than that to preserve the Communist system in the Soviet Union, to retain its hold over the numerous minorities which live between the Great Russians and their frontiers with the outside world, to retain its hold over the East European buffer states, and to prevent the seepage of too many Western notions of freedom into its own people. China on the other hand poses no threat whatsoever to the Soviet political structure as such, and is unlikely to exericse anything like the attraction for the Soviet Asian minorities that the West might still do for white inhabitants of the Soviet bloc.

So in the immediate and medium-term future Sino-Soviet relations may well continue a gradual improvement. If Moscow were able to find a solution it found acceptable to its Afghan and US problems, it would be in a position to go some way to meet current Chinese demands on frontier troop deployment or Kampuchea from a position of strength. The Soviet involvement in Afghanistan and Vietnam is directed as much against the United States as against China. Moreover, not the least obstacle in the way of any Soviet concessions on any front is Soviet public opinion and the desire of the Moscow government not to seem weak in the eyes of its own military and its own masses. But some Soviet yielding on Chinese demands, as a compliment to the similar needs of Beijing, could provide the catalyst for further concessions from China.

Materials for a Sino-Soviet deal are to hand at all times and may become more abundant as the years go by. The future ambitions of the Kremlin may well embrace Western Europe and the Middle East, politically fragmented areas where the Russians would not come into great conflict with China. The most obvious immediate area for the expansion of Chinese influence is Southeast Asia, with its large compatriot population, and this is a region in which Soviet interests are new and less than vital, except in the sense of trans-hemispheric sea-routes. But whether and how soon any deal might be concluded depends on the wearing away of suspicion, the policies and developments in the rest of the world and Chinese and Soviet estimations of their own strength.

This history has followed Sino-Russian relations from the earliest times to the end of 1982, and considered their prospects for the years fairly soon to come: it would seen tame to conclude without attempting some prognosis of their more distant future.

Historians have no more right than anyone else to claim clairvoyance, but perhaps uniquely amongst professionals our training accustoms us to look back down long vistas of years and pick out the contours of significant change over centuries and millenia. And since we are used to envisaging portentous developments occupying great timespans in the past, we are tempted to look at the key features of current world history and speculate as to the major trains of events which they may entail in the future. Bertrand de Jouvenel in *The Art of Conjecture* (London, 1967) points out the notorious unreliability of arguing from present data to the future, a process he compares to a work of art.

Succumbing to this temptation nevertheless, the present writer would support the view that China will be able to consolidate and maintain its independent role and become an increasingly great world power. Some predict China's collapse into regionalism again, in face of its aversion to a federal constitution seemingly more suited to a country of such size. But the stakes at issue for the Chinese people are too high, and their evident consciousness of their national prospects too keen, for collapse to seem a serious danger at the moment. China's long-term interest seems to lie towards closer ties with Japan, in view of its immense technological potential, proximity and cultural compatibility, and China's probable capacity to supply Japan with oil: a Sino-Japanese partnership would be well-nigh unbeatable. History has shown us that the leading centres of the world are forever changing. The economic statistics tell their own story, whilst on a more subjective plane anyone who has seen the tremendous pace of development in Japan, Taiwan and Hong Kong, amongst the Southeast Asian Chinese and in Korea over these last ten or twenty years, and now sees China beginning to gain momentum, will find it easy to believe that it is here that a new nucleus of power is being forged. At the same time, the difficulties encountered by the Chinese bureaucratic machine in adjusting to modernisation are considerable, and mean that China cannot proceed at the speed of the smaller East Asian units.

Much in Sino-Russian relations will depend on what happens in the United States. A features of the present American scene ominously suggestive of future decline is the tendency on the part of many large companies to invest more in production abroad than at home. Other long-term trends there, as envisaged by realistic American observers, seem to indicate a great inflow of Latin Americans and other non-white groups, increased inter-communal rivalry and thus more and more attention focused on domestic rather than foreign affairs. Already the presidential election system is perceived by America's allies as a substantial stumbling block to the conduct of a good foreign policy, but seems to be incapable of reform for reasons of internal politics. Should this drift continue, the attention of other powers may be directed more to influencing American policy from within. The Soviet grain purchases have already been cited as a minor example of this, and in the future the emergence of a sufficiently strong Chinese minority in the United States may easily make it as impossible for Washington to follow a really anti-China policy as it already is for it to follow policies which are entirely against the interests of Israel or the Black African countries.

Should China again relapse into civil strife such a picture would of course be altered, but the possibility of promoting its world influence through strong Chinese communities overseas is in the long run a very real one for a nation of China's stupendous numbers. The Russians have not the faintest chance of doing the same. Of all the powers, China is richest in the greatest resource of all—people of one ethnic group of proud traditions and demonstrated gifts, and this should ensure its survival as a state, if not its rise to dominance over the present super-powers. China's position also looks stronger in so far as its low standard of living will help it to survive more easily the economic problems which threaten the developed countries, although the Soviet Union too should be able to live through any major crisis of capitalism more or less intact.

Demographic factors bid fair to play an increasing role in Soviet affairs. Unless by striking technological advances the Soviet government could somehow make it economically attractive for Russian women to produce large families, the Russians as an ethnic group may have to absorb more of the other groups into the power structure and indeed may not be able to hold their own against a massive and rising East Asian power bloc. Muslim birthrates are however beginning to decline. Moreover, Moscow might be able to bolster its position by extending its control over Western Europe should the precarious moves there towards political unity fail, economic troubles worsen, and American leadership fall short. But if such a hegemony were not established with goodwill by a more liberal Soviet Union, it would be a source of weakness rather than strength unless relations between Europe and Asian states become much exacerbated. (This could come about through the rise of China, or excessive pressure for immigration into Europe from the Third World, which might follow the model of the present struggle against illegal immigrants into Hong Kong on a much larger scale.) A Soviet domination over the Middle East would be fraught with even more risks for the stability of the Russian position in view of the already large Muslim minorities within the Union.

Sooner or later change must come to the present Soviet system, if for no other reason than the growing sophistication and education of its people. In an optimistic scenario, this could happen within the one-party state by modifications in the direction of rule of law, freedom of speech, and constitutional mechanisms for the replacement of leadership at all levels. In this way the advantages of the Soviet and Western systems could be to some extent combined, providing a basis for more constructive and positive Soviet leadership over Europe. In a pessimistic scenario, economic chaos or defeat in war would provide the most likely setting, as in 1917, for a ghastly denouement, with the break-up of the state and possible cession of territories to China.

Whatever happens, a very long time may elapse before the Russians and Chinese can live together politically in total brotherly love, and in the meanwhile both they and the rest of us exist in the shadow of ecological problems and under the black cloud of the nuclear threat, hanging today particularly over the Soviet Union and the United States, but liable to hang tomorrow more heavily over the Soviet Union and China as well.

Bibliographical guide

Chapters 1 and 2: China and Russia until 1618

There is not a large selection of histories of China in English in print at the present time. A sound introduction to the history of all pre-modern East Asia is provided by Edwin O. Reischauer *East Asia: the great tradition* Harvard University Press, several editions including paperback. An up-to-date history of China alone by a French scholar has recently been translated into English: *A history of China* by Jacques Gernet, Cambridge University Press, 1982. Both these books are expensive, even the paperback of Reischauer, but are highly recommendable.

A variety of paperbacks are much cheaper but of less solid value. *China; a short cultural history* by C.P. Fitzgerald, Cresset Press, several editions, is colourful and informative on the facet indicated. *A history of China* by Wolfram Eberhard, Routledge and Kegan Paul, is weak on foreign affairs and the 4th revised 1977 edition needs updating in the light of much modern research, but it is convenient and inexpensive.

Joseph Needham's monumental history of science and technology in China is being summarised in small paperbacks by Colin A. Ronan as *The shorter science and civilization in China* Cambridge University Press. Two volumes of this series have so far appeared. A critique of Needham's work is provided by Nakayama and Sivin (eds) *Chinese science* MIT Press, 1973.

On the Russian side, two tried favourites among many histories written in the last 30 years are Lionel Kochan's *Making of Modern Russia* Pelican (new edition said to be in preparation) and Nicholas Riasanovsky's *History of Russia* Oxford University Press, several editions.

This introductory material should launch the reader into the rivers of work on both countries in their pre-Communist periods.

Chapters 3 and 4: 1618–1725

The only other fairly full history of Sino-Russian relations is O.E. Clubb, *The History of Sino-Russian Relations: The Great Game* Columbia University Press, 1971.

The classic work for Sino-Russian relations from 1618 to 1725 is Mark Mancall's *Russia and China* Harvard University Press, 1971. One might say that it is the classic work so far on any period of the relations before 1917, for it combines a mastery of Russian and Chinese sources and of the European background which is unrivalled. Yet this is a first-generation work of modern scholarship, and the complexities of the field are such that even this needs updating. Apart from a very few thin patches in the text, just after it was completed a collection of hitherto-unpublished documents on the period was brought out in the Soviet Union: N.F. Demidova and V.S. Miasnikov, (ed) L.I. Duman *Russko-kitaiskie otnosheniia v 17-om veke* Moscow, vol. 1 1969, vol. 2 1973. Another interesting Soviet book on the subject appeared at the same time: V.A. Aleksandrov *Rossiia na dalnevostochnykh rubezhakh* Moscow, 1969. Whilst these Soviet books do not alter the validity of Mancall's, they do contain some fresh material which he could have incorporated with advantage, especially regarding the Milovanov mission and the Ghantimur affair. These were re-interpreted more convincingly in the light of the Soviet documents by Eric Widmer (see his article in *Ch'ing-shih wen-t'i* vol. 2, no. 4, November 1970). In his book *The Russian ecclesiastical mission in Peking in the 18th century* Harvard University Press, 1977, Widmer also produced some other fresh interpretations of events in the period 1689-1727, for which Mancall had provided the groundwork.

Earlier books on this period in English and French which are well-worth reading by afficionados of the subject are John F. Baddeley *Russia, Mongolia and China* 2 vols, London, 1919, and Gaston Cahen *Histoire des relations de la Russie avec la Chine sous Pierre le Grand* Paris, 1911. Both are available in major libraries.

Chapter 5: 1725-1792

The eighteenth century, from 1727 to 1792, is the last great stretch of Sino-Russian relations on which no fundamental modern research has yet been published. Until recently it had defied scholars, partly because of the paucity of materials available in Russian and more especially in Chinese, and partly because of the linguistic barriers. Any satisfactory history would have to take account of the contemporary relations between China, Russia and the Mongols, and hence incorporate sources in Mongol, if not in Manchu, as well as the other languages involved. Consequently, after Mancall's work ends in 1727, the eighteenth century remains sketchily covered, a fact reflected in the present chapter which is forced to rely more on narrative than interpretation.

The most useful modern work on this period is Clifford M. Foust's *Muscovite and Mandarin: Russia's trade with China and its setting, 1727-1805* University of North Carolina Press, Chapel Hill, 1969. This most competent study of the commercial relations also provides a convenient outline of the political relations but does not treat these in depth, nor does it use much in the way of Chinese sources. Eric Widmer's study of the ecclesiastical mission again does not go much beyond the bounds of mission activities after 1727, and is at its best in re-interpreting and enriching the ground covered by Mancall to 1727.

Chapters 6 and 7: 1792-1860

The reader is referred in the first place to Volume X Part 1 of the *Cambridge History of Modern China* Cambridge Univeristy Press, 1979; chapter 7 by Joseph Fletcher is entitled 'Sino-Russian relations 1800-1862'. Fletcher refers — more extensively it seems than his footnotes indicate — to my book *The Expansion of Russia in East Asia 1857-1860* University of Malaya Press, Kuala Lumpur, 1968, which has an introductory chapter on 1792-1857. (A Chinese translation of this was published in Beijing in 1979.) Fletcher's chapter is in general much better and more up-to-date than my book, though the latter contains a good deal of detail, particularly from the Russian side, which Fletcher's shorter China-based chapter does not need to mention. I also published an article in the *Journal of Asian Studies* February 1970, entitled 'Further light on the expansion of Russia in East Asia 1792-1860', to which he does not refer.

Fletcher, professor of Chinese at Harvard, is one of the academic world's foremost linguists and one of the few equipped to tackle the study of Sino-Russian relations in this period and in the neglected eighteenth century. It is much to be hoped that he will turn his enormous gifts to further historical research in this area.

Chapter 8: 1860-1917

Although the highlights of this period have been made the subject of various studies since the Second World War, there are still no really adequate accounts of these years in English. The late George Lensen's posthumously published two-volume work *Balance of intrigue: international rivalry in Korea and Manchuria 1884-1899* University Presses of Florida, 1982, is a valuable contribution but unfortunately does not get directly at the best Chinese sources. A.L. Narochnitskii's *Kolonial'naia politika kapitalisticheskikh derzhav na Dal'nem Vostoke 1860-1895* Moscow, 1956, is useful, written from a Soviet-Marxist stand.

There is a valuable study of the Ili affair by Immanuel Hsu *The Ili crisis* Oxford Univeristy Press, 1965. For the years 1881-1904 there is A. Malozemoff's good *Russian Far Eastern policy 1881-1904* Berkeley, 1958 — much less detailed than Lensen's work. P.H.S. Tang deals rather briefly with *Russian and Soviet policy in Manchuria and Outer Mongolia 1911-1931* Durham, 1959, writing from the viewpoint of a Chinese patriot. The early Soviet historian B.A. Romanov's *Rossiia v Man'chzhurii* Moscow, 1928, is still a precious source of first-hand policy information, being based entirely on the archives of the tsarist Ministry of Finance. It is written from an anti-tsarist, Marxist internationalist stance that contrasts remarkably with the later attitudes of Soviet historians. The English translation by Susan Wilbur Jones under the title *Russia in Manchuria* Ann Arbor, 1954, is not 100 per cent the same as the original, though in general a faithful translation.

Local Sino-Russian relations in Manchuria have been the subject of or are touched upon in several books: Chao Chung-fu *Qing-ji Zhong-E Dong-san-sheng jie-wu jiao-she* Taipei, 1970; R.H.Y. Lee *The Manchurian frontier in the Ching dynasty* Harvard University Press, 1970; M.H. Hunt *Frontier defence and the Open Door: Manchuria in Chinese-American relations 1895-1911* Yale University Press, 1973; R.K.I. Quested *'Matey' imperialists? The tsarist Russians in Manchuria 1895-1917* Centre of Asian Studies, University of Hong Kong, 1982.

Russian activities in the Kashgar area of Sinkiang are mentioned in C.P. Skrine and P. Nightingale's *Macartney in Kashgar* Methuen, 1973.

A deep study of Russia's intellectual influence on Chinese thinkers is Don C. Prince *Russia and the roots of the Chinese revolution 1896-1911* Harvard University Press, 1974.

Finally there are some articles and smaller studies on various parts of the years after 1895: R.K.I. Quested and N. Tsuji (for the Japanese sources) 'A fresh look at the Sino-Russian conflict of 1900 in Manchuria' *Journal of the Institute of Chinese Studies of the Chinese University of Hong Kong* 9, 2, 1978, pp. 473-501; R.K.I. Quested *The Russo-Chinese Bank: a multinational financial base of Tsarism in China 1895-1910* Birmingham Slavonic Monographs no. 2, Birmingham, *1977;* R.K.I. Quested 'An introduction to the enigmatic career of Chou Mien' *Journal of Oriental Studies* 16, 1 & 2, 1978 (Chou Mien was a leading collaborator of the Russians in Manchuria).

Thus it can be seen that although this period has been better served than the eighteenth century, there remains a need for solid studies in English of the political and indeed economic relations. Readers should look out for work by Howard Spendelowe, a Harvard post-graduate who has been studying the 1895-1904 span for some years. An important study focussed mainly on Russo-Japanese relations is also forthcoming by Ian Nish.

Chapter 9: 1917-1943

The revolutions of 1911 and 1917 in China and Russia ushered in a new historical epoch which has attracted much more attention from historians. A great deal has already been published on Sino-Soviet relations of this period, much of it so soon after the events as to rank as contemporary commentary or the raw materials of history, rather than historiography in the real sense of the word. It will be decades, at the very least, before anyone can approach this recent period with the authority and detachment of Mancall.

Readers approaching either Russia or China for the first time may be directed to the following general introductory histories: James E. Sheridan *China in disintegration: the Republican era in Chinese history, 1912-1949* Free Press, New York, 1975; Li Chien-nung *The political history of China 1840-1928* Stanford University Press, 1956 and reprints; R.C. Thornton *China: the struggle for power 1917-1972* Indiana University Press, 1973; H. Carrère d'Encausse *A history of the Soviet Union 1917-53* Longmans, 1981; and J.P. Nettl *The Soviet achievement* Thames and Hudson, 1967 for differing views.

For Lenin, one could well start with L. Schapiro and P. Reddaway (ed.) *Lenin: the man, the theorist, the leader: a a reappraisal* Pall Mall Press, 1967, and proceed perhaps to D. Shub *Lenin* Pelican, several editions, or A. Ulam *Lenin and the Bolsheviks* Secker and Warburg, 1966 and reprints (less sympathetic views). To get to grips with Lenin's thought, the most thorough and persuasive study so far is N. Harding *Lenin's political thought* vols 1 & 2,

MacMillan, 1977-81. There is no great biography of Lenin.
For Stalin, a good introduction would be T. Rigby *Stalin: an anthology* Prentice Hall, 1966, and *The Stalin dictatorship* Sydney University Press, 1968. A. Ulam *Stalin: the man and his era* Allen Lane, 1974, is readable, and R.C. Tucker's biography, of which the first volume only has appeared, promises to be the most definitive: *Stalin as revolutionary 1879-1929* W.W. Norton, New York, 1973. Also recommended is R.C. Tucker (ed.) *Stalinism: essays in historical interpretation (the Bellagio conference)* Norton, 1977. Stalin's thought is also discussed by R.C. Tucker in *The Soviet political mind* Allen & Unwin, 1972.

Returning to the direct Sino-Soviet scene, a useful book in Russian is M.I. Sladkovskii *Istoriia torgovo-ekonomicheskikh otnoshenii S.S.S.R. s Kitaem 1917-74* Moscow, 1977. A classic study on the relations in Manchuria and between Sun Yatsen, the Peking government and Moscow is S.T. Leong *Sino-Soviet diplomatic relations 1917-1926* Australian National University Press, 1976. Alan S. Whiting *Soviet policies in China 1917-24* Stanford University Press, 1954 and 1968, is still of some interest, though mostly superseded by Leong's book.

For the relations between Sun Yatsen and Moscow, there is Dan Jacob's highly readable biography of Borodin, the chief Soviet political adviser to Sun — *Borodin* Harvard University Press, 1980) — but this uses no Chinese sources. There is also a slim book by Leng and Palmer *Sun Yatsen and Communism* Praeger, 1960, which is a useful supplement. The standard biographies of Sun by Harold Schiffrin and Martin Wilbur rather downplay the Soviet dimension. There is also an interesting chapter on Soviet aid to the KMT by R. Lowenthal in Royal Institute of International Affairs *The impact of the Russian Revolution 1917-67* Oxford University Press, 1967.

A number of former Soviet advisers have published memoirs, of which the most notable is General A.I. Cherepanov *Zapiski voennogo sovetnika v Kitae* Moscow, 1964. Dieter Heinzig in West Germany published a monograph on these advisers in German in 1978; it is now out of print and has not been translated.

For the Chinese Communist movement, J.P. Harrison's *The Long March to power, 1921-72* Praeger, 1972, is highly recommended. The history of the Chinese Communist Party has been clarified in stages, and Harrison has tied together most of the major discoveries made until 1972. He had access to Ilpyong J. Kim's thesis on the Jiangxi Soviet, but the revised published version of this appeared later than Harrison's book as *The politics of Chinese Communism: Kiangsi under the Soviets* University of California Press, 1973. More work on the Returned Students is awaited from Shum Kwee Kwong in Australia.

The problem of the United Front and Stalin's and Trotsky's policies towards it is treated in C. Brandt *Stalin's failure in China* Harvard Univeristy Press, 1958 and subsequent paperback edition by Norton, and *Leon Trotsky on China* Monad Press, 1976. (The earlier *Problems of the Chinese revolution* by Leon Trotsky, introducted by Max Schachter, Paragon, 1966, is not complete.)

For Mao, Dick Wilson (ed.) *Mao Tse-tung in the scales of history* Cambridge University Press, 1977, or Stuart Schram *Mao Tse-tung* Pelican, several editions, is a good initial approach. On Mao's thought, the most fundamental works are Frederic Wakeman *History and Will* University of California Press, 1973, and

J.B. Starr *Continuing the Revolutions: the political thought of Mao Tse-tung* Princeton University Press, 1979. For the CCP–Soviet relations in the Li Lisan period there is R.C. Thornton *The Comintern and the Chinese Communists, 1928-31* University of Washington Press, 1969. Some detailed studies of parts or aspects of the relations in the second United Front period which appeared after J.P. Harrison's book are: G. Benton 'The second Wang Ming line' *China Quarterly* no. 61, March 1975, pp. 61-94; J.D. Armstrong *Revolutionary diplomacy: Chinese foreign policy and the United Front doctrine* University of California Press, 1980; *P.P.* Vladimirov *The Vladimirov Diaries* Hale, London, 1979. Relations between Moscow and a warlord of the 1920s are discussed in J.E. Sheridan *Chinese warlord: the career of Feng Yu-hsiang* Stanford University Press, 1966.

There are no special studies in English on the relationship between the KMT and the Russians after the death of Sun Yatsen. But on the Soviet side we have A.M. Dubinskii *Sovetsko-kitaiskie otnosheniia v periode iapono-kitaiskoi voiny 1937-45* Moscow, Mysl', 1980. There are also various works in Chinese published in Taiwan, but none of them has attracted much scholarly appraisal in the West. Western and overseas Chinese scholars have been reluctant to embark on the relations with the KMT for a variety of reasons.

There are two books which provide memoirs of the Soviet universities for Chinese and other foreigners: Yueh Sheng *The Sun Yatsen University in Moscow and the Chinese revolution* Center for Asian Studies, University of Kansas, 1971, and Wang Fanhsi *Chinese revolutionary: memoirs 1919-1949* translated and introduced by Gregor Benton, Oxford University Press, 1980.

For Manchuria, George Lensen's *The damned inheritance: Sino-Russian diplomatic relations over Manchuria 1924-35* is introductory and rather pro-Soviet. For a general survey of policy relations on the CER there is Chang Tao-shing *Russia, China and the C.E.R.* Hoover Institution Press, 1973. John Stephan's *The Russian Fascists: tragedy and farce in exile* Harper Row, 1978, is a brilliant piece of sugar-coated research on one facet of White Russian life in Manchuria.

The present writer may be publishing a general survey of Soviet and White Russian local activities in Manchuria from 1917, but a more important work to await is that of Felix Patrikeev, who is completing an Oxford thesis on Soviet policy in Manchuria from 1924-1931.

For Xinjiang, the best introductory work is L.E. Nyman *Great Britain, and Chinese, Russian and Japanese interests in Sinkiang 1918-34* Lund, Esselte Studium, 1977. In its conclusion this extends to 1945.

Chapter 10: 1943–1950

For the origins of the Sino-Soviet alliance there is again no detailed study as yet. A multitude of secondary works have been devoted to Sino-US and Soviet-US relations, to list which would be tedious.

J. Rearden-Anderson *Yenan and the great powers: the origins of Communist China's foreign policy 1944-46* Columbia University Press, 1980, comes the closest so far to plotting the stages by which Mao came to terms with Stalin, but lacks Chinese language sources, let alone archival material.

Two Soviet books yield a good deal to careful reading: O.B. Borisov and B.T. Koleskov *Sino-Soviet relations 1945-70* edited and introduced by Vladimir Petrov, Indiana University Press, 1975 (another translation by Yuri Shirokov appeared in Moscow, in 1975 and the original was published in Moscow in 1971 under the title *Sovetsko-kitaiskie otnosheniia 1945-70: kratkii ocherk)* and O.B. Borisov *Sovetskii Soiuz i Man'chzhurskaia revoliutsionnaia basa* Moscow, 1975. This is shorter, but contains some information not in the longer book. Several later editions of the latter carry the story later.

Those interested in getting to the bottom of Sino-Soviet relations in this period, especially in Manchuria, should watch keenly for work to appear by Stephen Levine. So far one may consult his chapter 'Soviet-American rivalry in Manchuria and the Cold War' in Hsueh Chun-tu (ed.) *Dimensions of China's foreign relations* Praeger, 1977, and his PhD thesis, *Political integration in Manchuria*, Harvard University, 1972 — a deceptively vague title for an important study. In these studies Levine by implication disregards Jiang Kaishek's own account of his relations with Stalin over Manchuria, given in *Soviet Russia and China: a summing-up at seventy* Farrar, Strauss and Girar, New York, 1975. However, this is worth reading and is partially at least borne out by indications in Sladkovskii's book on the economic relations between China and the Soviet Union.

A useful background work on the Chinese civil war is Suzanne Pepper *Civil War in China: the political struggle 1945-49* University of California Press, 1978. It does not touch much on Manchuria.

Chapter 11 and 12: 1950–1969

The alliance still awaits an authoritative study, and the 1960s are even worse served historiographically. The whole period from 1950 can only be approached through a variety of books which touch on it. General histories of Chinese and Soviet foreign policy are essential ingredients and of these two studies can be recommended as a start: A. Ulam *Expansion and co-existence: the history of Soviet foreign policy 1917-73* Praeger, 1974, and Harold Hinton *China's turbulent quest: an analysis of China's foreign relations since 1949* Indiana University Press, 2nd ed., 1973. Both works contain interpretations which have been challenged and which in Hinton's case have been modified by the author himself, but both are very readable. Ulam is not always totally accurate on details of Sino-Soviet relations. A.I. Rubinstein *Soviet foreign policy since World War II: imperial and global* Winthrop, 1981, brings a different perspective to Ulam's.

It is interesting to note the changes in attitudes of American historians towards the Soviet Union between the late 1960s and the early 1980s. A Britisher may well find Robin Edmonds *Soviet foreign policy 1962-73* Oxford University Press, 1975, 2nd ed. 1977, more congenial in standpoint, and hope that there will be a further instalment. Another essential book by a British author on Chinese foreign policy is Michael Yahuda's *China's role in world affairs* St Martin's Press, New York, 1978.

Having read the general foreign policy works, one may proceed via a look at Clubb to Sladkovskii's economic history, which may be compared with Cheng

Chu-yuan's *Economic relations between China and Russia, 1950-60* Praeger, 1964 — Cheng being an overseas Chinese scholar with an entirely different viewpoint.

For military relations, there are R. Garthoff *Sino-Soviet military relations* Praeger, 1966 and W. Clemens *The arms race and Sino-Soviet relations* Hoover Institution Press, 1968. M. Halperin *Sino-Soviet relations and arms control* MIT Press, 1967, seems more dated.

On the Korean War there are many works advancing different interpretations of the Sino-Soviet involvement. A good, old study by Alan Whiting *China crosses the Yalu* MacMillan, 1960, may be compared to newer ones like R.R. Simmons *The strained alliance: Peking, Pyongyang and the politics of the Korean War* Free Press, New York, 1975, and Gavin McCormack *Crisis in Korea* Bertrand Russell Peace Foundation, Nottingham, 1977.

J.P. Harrison, and still more Bill Brugger's *Contemporary China* Croom Helm, 1977, are invaluable for sorting out the internal history of Communist China, in which the Soviet presence loomed so much greater than China's did in the Soviet Union. Jurgen Domes *The internal politics of China 1949-70* Stuttgart, 1971 (English translation by Hurst, 1973) is a slightly older analysis that differs in certain respects from Brugger.

There is useful information on aspects of the 1960s in Douglas T. Stuart and William T. Tow *China, the Soviet Union and the West: strategic and political dimensions in the 1980s* Westview, 1981.

There is nothing on Manchuria for this period apart from the book by Borisov, but for Xinjiang there is a very interesting work by D. McMillen *Chinese Communist power and policy in Xinjiang 1949-1977* Westview, 1979. Already rare, but important, is G. Moseley *The Ili Kazakh Autonomous Chou: a Sino-Soviet cultural frontier* Harvard University Press, 1966.

For the final break-up of the alliance, by far the most detailed is D. Zagoria *The Sino-Soviet conflict, 1958-1961* Princeton University Press, 1962, and an admirable very detailed study, William E. Griffith *The Sino-Soviet Rift; 1962-63* MIT Press, 1964. Both these works naturally lack the perspective of those published recently.

The closest study of the border dispute and the Damanskii island fighting of 1969 is the article by Thomas W. Robinson 'The Sino-Soviet border dispute: background, development and the 1969 clashes' *American Political Science Review* no. 66, December 1972.

One of the greatest difficulties is to establish a clear picture of Sino-Soviet rivalry in the Third World. For the Soviet side, for the period from the death of Stalin to 1970, there are the excellent books by Charles B. McLane — *Soviet-Asian relations, Soviet Middle Eastern relations,* and *Soviet-African relations* Central Asia Research Centre, 1973. These purvey plain, solid information, a most refreshing change from the woolly commentary offered by some writers on this subject. McLane commendably adds some information about Chinese ties with some of the key countries, but on the whole there is nothing similar for the Chinese relations. One can turn to a few more detailed books for help: B.A. Larkin *China and Africa 1949-70: the foreign policy of the P.R.C.* University of California Press, 1971; Y. Shichor *The Middle East in China's foreign policy 1949-77;* H.S.H. Behbehani *China's foreign policy in the Arab world, 1955-75;* W.R. Smyser *The independent Vietnamese, Vietnamese Communism between*

Russia and China 1956-69 Center for International Studies, Ohio University, 1980; and Jan Taylor *China and Southeast Asia: Peking's relations with revolutionary movements* Praeger, 1976. A.Z. Rubinstein *Soviet and Chinese influence in the Third World* Praeger, 1975, is disappointingly vague on many scores.

Chapters 13 and 14: since 1969

For the years since 1969 Stuart and Tow's book already cited is an indispensable introduction, and equally so *The Sino-Soviet Conflict: a global perspective* (ed.) Herbert J. Ellison, University of Washington Press, 1982. But even the latter does not deal entirely satisfactorily with the rivalry in the Third World, omitting particularly any discussion of Southeast Asia outside Vietnam, and Africa. Kenneth G. Lieberthal's *Sino-Soviet conflict in the 1970s: its evolution and implications for the strategic triangle* Rand, 1978, gives useful details about the direct negotiations in the early 1970s. David Rees' *Soviet border problems: China and Japan* Institute for the Study of Conflict, 1982, deals with its subject down to 1978. Robert H. Donaldson (ed.) *The Soviet Union and the Third World: successes and failures* Westview, 1981, is helpful for many areas, but not very enlightening on Africa. W. Weinstein's *Soviet and Chinese aid to African nations* Praeger, 1980 steps into the gap.

List of Chinese dynasties, Qing emperors and Russian tsars

Chinese dynasties

Shang	1028 BC
Zhou	1028-221 BC
Qin	221 BC-206 BC
Han	200 BC-200 AD
Division	200-581
Sui	581-618
Tang	618-906
Sung	906-1179
Mongol	1234-1368
Ming	1368-1644
Qing	1644-1911
Warlord period	1911-1928
Nationalist	1928-1949
Chinese People's Republic	1949-

Reign titles of Qing emperors

Shunzhi	1644
Kangxi	1662
Yungzheng	1722
Qianlong	1735
Jiaqing	1796
Daoguang	1821
Xienfeng	1851
Tongzhi	1861
Guangxu	1875
Xuantong	1908

Russian tsars of the Romanov dynasty

Mikhail	1614–1645
Aleksei	1645–1676
Fedor	1676–1682
Regent Sophia	1682–1689
Peter the Great	1689–1725
Catherine I	1725–1727
Peter II	1727–1730
Anna	1730–1741
Elizabeth	1741–1762
Peter III	1762
Catherine II	1762–1796
Paul	1796–1801
Alexander I	1801–1825
Nicholas I	1825–1855
Alexander II	1855–1881
Alexander III	1881–1894
Nicholas II	1894–1917

SINO–RUSSIAN RELATIONS : 20th CENTURY

	RUSSIA	CHINA	SOME CROSS REFERENCES
1911		Sun Yatsen Revolution	
1914			First World War
1917	Revolution		
1920	1918–20 Civil War	Founding of CCP	
1924	Lenin dies	First United Front Soviet-KMT Treaty	
1927	December: Stalin supreme Trotsky exiled		
1929	First 5-year plan Collectivisation of agriculture	End of First United Front Sino/Soviet border war in Manchuria Nationalist government Nationalist–Soviet relations broken off	Great Depression
1932		Japan occupies Manchuria Resumption of Nationalist–Soviet relations	
1933		Soviet influence established in Xinjiang	Hitler comes to power in Germany
1934	Stalin's great Terror begins	Long March	
1935		Stalin sells CER to Japan CCP HQ in Yenan	
1936		Second United Front	
1939	Soviet–Japanese battle of Nomonhan		Germany invades Poland

	RUSSIA	CHINA	SOME CROSS REFERENCES
1941	German invasion		Pearl Harbour
1942		Soviet withdrawal from Xinjiang	
1945		Soviet invasion of Manchuria	Victory over Germany & Japan Atomic bomb on Hiroshima
1946		Soviet army withdraws from Manchuria Civil War begins	
1949		Communist Victory	
1950	Sino/Soviet alliance		Korean War starts
1953	Stalin dies		
1956	Krushchev denounces Stalin		
1957	Sputnik Hydrogen bomb	Great Leap Forward	Treaty of Rome
1960	Withdrawal of Soviet specialists from China		
1963	Start of Sino–Soviet Cold War		US/Soviet/Britain partial test ban treaty White House– Kremlin Hotline
1964	Brezhnev succeeds Khrushchev	Nuclear test	
1965	Soviet military aid to Vietnam		Escalation of Vietnam War
1967		Cultural Revolution	
1968	Soviet invasion of Czechoslovakia Brezhnev doctrine		
1969		Ussuri Island clash	
1970			Soviet–West German treaty

	RUSSIA	CHINA	SOME CROSS REFERENCES
1971		Lin Biao affair Nixon's visit	Britain signs Treaty of Rome
1973	Brezhnev visits US		US leaves Vietnam
1975			Fall of South Vietnam
1976		Death of Mao Fall of Gang of Four	
1978		Sino–Japanese Treaty US & China exchange ambassadors Sino-Vietnam War	Pro-Soviet coup in Afghanistan Revolution in Iran
1980	Soviet army in Afghanistan	New peasant policies completed	
	Death of Brezhnev Succession of Andropov	New foreign policy line	

SINO-RUSSIAN RELATIONS : 17th—20th CENTURIES

	RUSSIA	CHINA	SINO-RUSSIAN	SOME CROSS REFERENCES
1614	Romanov dynasty	Decline of Ming		
1618			First Russian mission to Peking	
1620				Mayflower
1644		Qing dynasty		
1662		Kangxi Emperor		*17th Century*
1656			Baikov mission	Civil War in England
1688			Fall of Albazin	Louis XIV in France
1689	Peter the Great		Treaty of Nerchinsk	
1692		*1692–1757* Conquest of Mongols	Trade regulations established	
Early 18th Century	Conquest of Baltic outlet			
1723	Start of Modernisation	Death of Kangxi		
1725	Death of Peter the Great		Treaty of Kiakhta	
1736		Qianlong Emperor		
1760				Industrial Revolution starts in Britain

SINO-RUSSIAN RELATIONS : 17th—20th CENTURIES

	RUSSIA	CHINA	SINO-RUSSIAN	SOME CROSS REFERENCES
1762	Catherine the Great		Supplementary treaty of Kiakhta	
1777		*Later 18th century* Start of Qing decline Population rise		US Constitution
1789				French Revolution
1792				
1795		Death of Qianlong Emperor		
1812	Napoleon invades Russia			
1815				Treaty of Vienna
1842		First Opium War		
1854		Taiping Rebellion	*1854–60* Russia takes Amur	Crimean War
1860		*1857–60* Second Opium War	Treaty of Peking	
1861	Emancipation of Serfs			American Civil War
1871	Start of industrialisation			Unification of Germany

Year				
1897			Russia starts building CER	
1898			Russia takes Port Arthur Russia invades Manchuria	
1900		Boxer Rising		
1905	Russo–Japanese War		Russia withdraws from S. Manchuria	Russo–Japanese War
1911		Sun Yat-sen revolution		
1914				First World War

Index